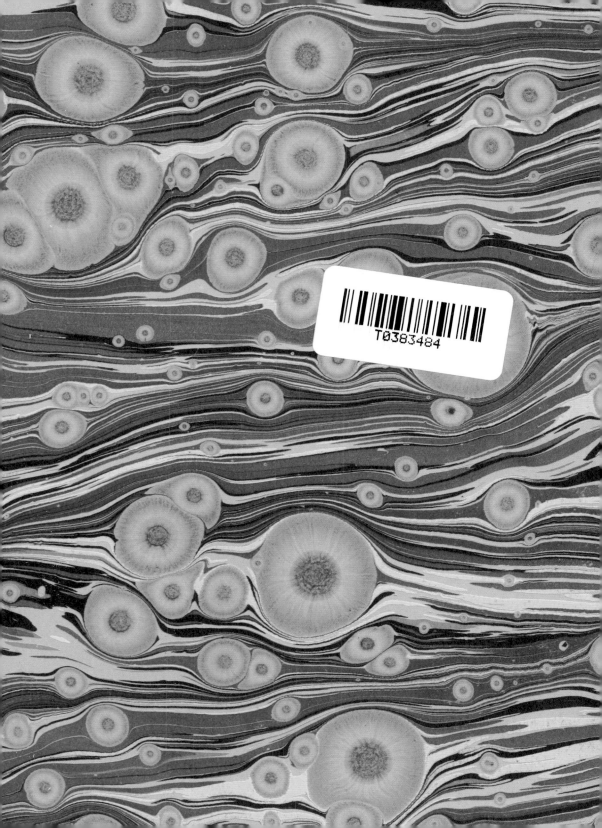

The Cosmic Dance

Finding patterns and pathways in a chaotic universe

Stephen Ellcock

Contents

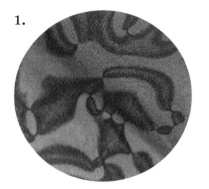
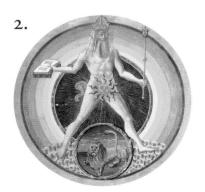

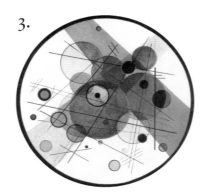

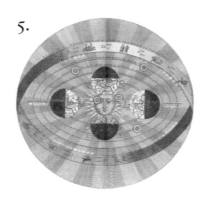

Preface — Regaining Perspective

An absence of perspective can be devastating in its consequences. It can, for example, lead to a situation in which the dominant species of a planet – the only one known to be inhabited – located in a remote backwater of the universe, can indulge in its darkest, most reckless and destructive impulses, plunging the world into chaos and threatening the very survival of its only home and the continued existence of every life form that has the misfortune to share the same sky and breathe the same air.

An absence of perspective can also prove incredibly destructive at a microcosmic, and altogether personal, level. It can, for example, lead a burnt-out, punch-drunk, middle-aged man to come apart at the seams, lose his bearings and find himself adrift in a world of pitfalls and unsprung traps, engaged in a perpetual war not only with himself but with friends and enemies, both real and imagined.

This book is the culmination of a decade-long attempt by that self-same middle-aged malcontent to come to terms with disorder and a feeling of insignificance and to re-engage with a world in which connections count and the occasional escape route still exists; a quest to find his place in space. This unlikely rehabilitation and reignited sense of purpose, ignited by an unforeseen chain of events and unanticipated interventions, also coincided with the unexpected reawakening of a lifelong, although lately dormant, obsession with the power of imagery, symbol and pattern.

Reconnection with the world of the image, via the gateway drug of early social media, swiftly evolved into an addiction that could only be satisfied by plunging into the infinite archive of images that was suddenly and freely available online. This unimaginably vast treasury, drawn from every conceivable place, culture and time, could now be accessed via the cracked screen of a reconditioned smartphone, or during frenetic, snatched 30-minute sessions in one of the long-vanished internet cafes of south-east London.

The contents of this book are but a tiny sample of the fruits of ceaseless foraging in the depths and darkest recesses of that treasury. Conceived as a journey from the microcosm to the macrocosm, *The Cosmic Dance* is a universal zoom, panning from microbe to metagalactic space, from quark to cosmos. Like Maria Sibylla Merian's exquisite studies of Suriname's indigenous insects, reptiles and flora, preserved in her astonishing book *Metamorphosis insectorum Surinamensium* (1705), it reveals natural cycles and relationships between living organisms and it highlights the interdependency that is a vital component of any functioning ecosystem on both a microscopic and a macrocosmic level.

Perspective can be recovered, even in the most unpromising of circumstances. In a world that is facing unprecedented peril and unimaginable challenges, the key to its survival is an acknowledgment of the beauty, purpose and patterns discernible in the universe; of the interconnectedness of all things; and of the need to restore balance. If we can somehow achieve this collective perspective then we may yet, in the words of William Carlos Williams, 'see with the eyes of angels'. △

△
William Carlos Williams, introduction to Allen Ginsberg's *Howl and Other Poems* (1959 edition), first published in 1956

○
Illustration from *Metamorphosis insectorum Surinamensium*, Maria Sibylla Merian, 1705

Introduction —
As Above, So Below

*'By looking down,
I see upward.
By looking up,
I see downward'* [△]

○
Illustration of Philosophy holding
the spheres from *De civitate Dei,*
Augustine of Hippo, translated
by Raoul de Presles, 15th century

△
Tycho Brahe, 1574

IT IS IN THE *Emerald Tablet*, a cryptic hermetic text dated to between *c.* 200 and 800 CE, attributed to the legendary Egyptian-Hellenistic figure Hermes Trismegistus, that the phrase 'as above, so below' derives. A translation of a later Latin version of the text gives the entire line as: 'That which is above is like to that which is below, and that which is below is like to that which is above, to accomplish the miracles of one thing.' In the West, during the medieval and Renaissance periods, it was thought that the *Emerald Tablet* was a summary of alchemical principles, containing instructions for turning base metals into gold and the secret of immortality. By the 16th century, however, the text was being interpreted by many, including occultist and alchemist John Dee (1527–1608/09), along more metaphysical lines with the 'one thing' being associated with the Platonic idea of *anima mundi* (world soul) in which the world

is viewed as a single living entity containing all other living entities and that all living things are connected. The modern counterpart to this idea is the Gaia hypothesis, proposed by scientist James Lovelock and biologist Lynn Margulis in 1974. Taking its name from the Greek goddess Gaia, the personification of Earth and mother of all life, the Gaia hypothesis contends that the Earth is a complex, self-regulating system in which living organisms have a synergistic relationship with their environment and the atmosphere, co-evolving with them. In this way the balance of the whole is maintained and optimal conditions for all life on the planet are perpetuated.

Since the ancient civilizations of Mesopotamia and Egypt, humankind has sought to comprehend how the universe came into being and to divine patterns and order within it. We have striven to understand the nature of humanity and our place in the universe. We have searched for correspondences between

○

□

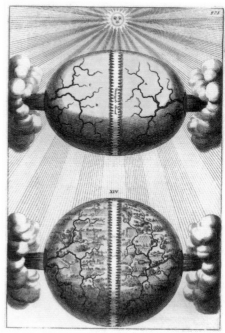

△
Creation of the Earth,
Wilhelm and Jan Goeree, 1690

the heavens and the Earth and between nature and the human body. And we have taken part in secret rituals in the hope of discovering the secrets of the universe, achieving spiritual enlightenment and immortality. The ancient Egyptian *ouroboros* symbol, depicting a snake or dragon coiling to eat its own tail, originally represented the cycle of life, death and rebirth, with the snake's process of shedding skin symbolizing the transmigration of souls. The term *ouroboros* is derived from ancient Greek, which translates as 'tail eating'. For the Gnostics, the *ouroboros* symbolized the unity of the divine and earthly in humanity, contrary forces coexisting at either end of the creature for eternity. In Hinduism the *ouroboros* symbolizes kundalini, or primal energy, and the endless cycle of life through reincarnation. The symbol can also be found in a document known as the *Chrysopoeia of Cleopatra* (3rd century CE) with the words 'the all is one' inscribed in the centre, attributed to Cleopatra the Alchemist. In alchemical terms it represents eternity and endless return. Alchemist Michael Maier (1568–1622), author of *Atalanta fugiens* (1618), names Cleopatra as one of only four female alchemists to have been able to create the philosopher's stone, a mythical substance – also known as the elixir of life – that was thought capable of turning base metals into gold and enabling immortality.

Did God create the universe out of nothing – *ex nihilo* – or out of chaos? Or did the universe emerge from a cosmic egg with the primordial being Pangu, who separated the opposing forces of yin and yang to form heaven and Earth as believed by the ancient Chinese? Were heaven and Earth formed by forcible separation of the primordial sky father, Rangi, and Earth

△

mother, Papa, bringing light to the world, as related in Māori mythology? Did the creator-beings of the Aboriginal Australians form the land, rivers, plants, animals, humans and sky of the Earth as they made their songlines, or dreaming tracks, across the land during the Dreaming? Every culture has a creation myth to explain how the universe came into being. In Shaivism, a tradition within Hinduism, Shiva (sometimes represented as the cosmic dancer Nataraja) is the supreme god, and brought the universe into being with a creation dance. He is usually depicted dancing within a circle of flames, which symbolizes his power to destroy the universe at will with a dance of destruction.

Evolution of Cosmos from a Single Point (Bindu), India, 18th century

Illustration of God creating the Earth, sun and moon from *Bible Historiale*, Guyart des Moulins, *c.* 1415

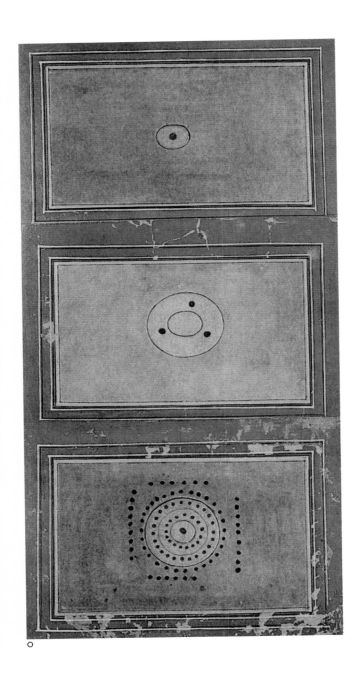

The Cosmic Dance

'Every thing that is in the heavens, on the
earth, and under the earth, is penetrated with
connectedness, is penetrated with relatedness.'

Hildegard von Bingen, quoted in *Meditations with Hildegard of Bingen*, 1982

○

○
The Eye That Sees Everything,
Man Ray, 1919

☐
The Creation of the Heavens,
Flemish, *c.* 1475

The Cosmic Dance

'Constantly regard the universe as one living being, having one substance and one soul; and observe how all things have reference to one perception, the perception of this one living being; and how all things act with one movement; and how all things are the cooperating causes of all things which exist.'

Marcus Aurelius, *Meditations*, c. 161–180 CE

According to the Vedic texts (*c.* 1300–900 BCE) which are the foundation of Hindu belief, the spirit of the divine being exists in all living things, and the self in every human being is the same as that in the supreme being. In the Chinese Daoist philosophical tradition, the *Dao*, or way, can be described as 'the flow of the universe'. Humankind is part of that flow and must act in harmony with the cycles and patterns of the universe. If an individual asserts their will against the natural rhythms of the universe, they may disrupt that harmony and the consequence of their action may be different from the one intended. Yin and yang must always be held in balance – when one rises, the other will fall. Yin and yang are bound together in one whole; each transforms the other. The

roots of Daoism can be found in the *I Ching*, or 'Book of Changes', a divination manual dating from 1000–750 BCE in which 64 named hexagrams, each with a short cryptic statement, can be consulted at random and interpreted to determine divine intent.

In ancient Greece, Plato (428/427–348/347 BCE) and the later neoplatonist philosophers attempted to define the relationship of human beings to the universe with the concept of microcosm and macrocosm. They viewed the individual human being as a little world (*mikros kosmos*), the composition and structure of which corresponded to that of the universe, or great world (*makros kosmos*). The original meaning of *kosmos* was 'order' and implied a harmonious and aesthetically beautiful arrangement of parts in any organic system. The concept of microcosmic and macrocosmic worlds is founded upon the idea that there is a universal similarity of pattern or structure from the largest scale to the smallest. Every living thing is a miniature, discrete world, complete in itself, whose composition and structure corresponds to that of the cosmos. Humanity is a reflection of the universe, containing all the essential elements present in the latter, a microcosm suspended in the matrix of the macrocosmos. Human nature is therefore reflected in the nature of the universe. The rules and forces governing all living organisms are the same as those shaping and governing the entire universe. Each simple substance is a living mirror of eternity and everything that happens in the macrocosm is reflected in the microcosm. For example, ancient Greek philosopher Empedocles (*c.* 494–434 BCE) postulated that four basic elements – air, fire, earth and water – made up all the structures

on Earth. Aristotle (384–322 BCE) later added
a fifth element, aether, or quintessence, a
sublime substance from which the stars were
made. These four earthly elements were later
aligned to the four humours, or vital bodily
fluids, identified by the father of Western
medicine, Hippocrates (*c.* 460–370 BCE),
as blood, yellow bile, black bile and phlegm.
The humours were thought by physician Galen
of Pergamon (129–*c.* 216 CE) to influence the
temperament of an individual – sanguine,
choleric, melancholic or phlegmatic – and
each was associated with a specific organ –
liver, gallbladder, spleen and brain or lungs.
The elements were also assigned to the signs
of the zodiac, relating to the twelve star
constellations; for example, Gemini is an
air sign, Leo a fire sign.

Galen also believed that diseased parts
or organs of the body could be treated by
plants or parts of plants that bore a likeness
to them. Jakob Böhme (1575–1624) developed
and communicated the concept widely, naming
it the doctrine of the signatures. Herbalist
Nicholas Culpeper (1616–1654) and botanist
William Coles (1626–1662) were ardent
proponents of the doctrine, believing that God
had endowed medicinal herbs with a physical
sign, or signature, of their therapeutic purpose.

Neoplatonist philosopher Plotinus (204/
205–270 CE) postulated that all matter and all
living beings could be placed in a hierarchical
structure that begins at the top with God
and finishes at the bottom with minerals; he
called it the great chain of being. Each form
in the hierarchy shares a characteristic with
the previous form, so the chain presents a
gradation of every kind of thing in existence
in the universe. Developed further during the

medieval period, the key segments of the chain
were: God, followed by the angels (spirit only),
followed by humans, animals and then plants
(a combination of spirit and matter), and finally
at the base of the chain minerals (matter only).

The ancient Greek philosophers surmised
that, as every form in the chain was linked to
the next, transmutation from one kind of thing
to another must be possible. They believed
that the *prima materia*, or first matter of the
universe, could be worked upon to create
the philosopher's stone, which could then be
used to turn base metals into gold and achieve
immortality. Greco-Egyptian alchemist and
Gnostic mystic Zosimos of Panopolis (*fl.* 300 CE)
authored the earliest known books on alchemy.
He held that the transmutation of lead into

THE COSMIC EGG, or world egg, features in the creation stories
of many Indo-European cultures. The idea first appeared in
Sanskrit scriptures, where it is known as *Brahmanda*, a conflation
of 'creator god' and 'egg'. In this version, the universe hatches
from the egg, breaking into two to form the heavens and the Earth.
In Chinese mythology, the universe and the deity Pangu both
form within a cosmic egg, which Pangu breaks open, separating
yin from yang and creating the heavens and the Earth. In the
ancient Greek Orphic tradition, the hermaphroditic deity Phanes
hatches out of the egg and immediately creates other gods.

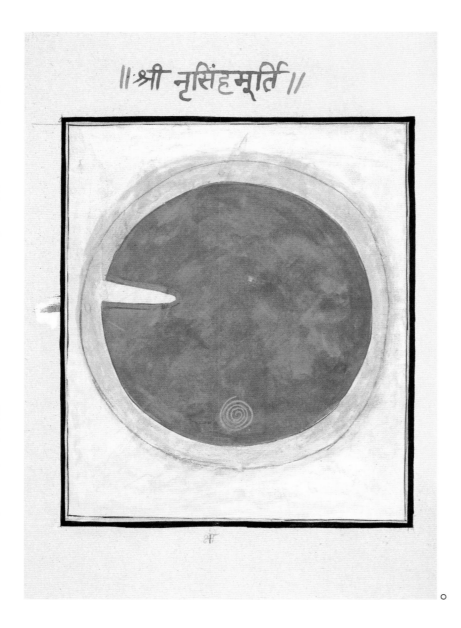

Shaligram painted by Badrinath Pandit,
Rajasthan, India, c. 1960

Series of *Brahmandas*, or cosmic eggs,
Northern India, 20th century

Introduction: *As Above, So Below*

19

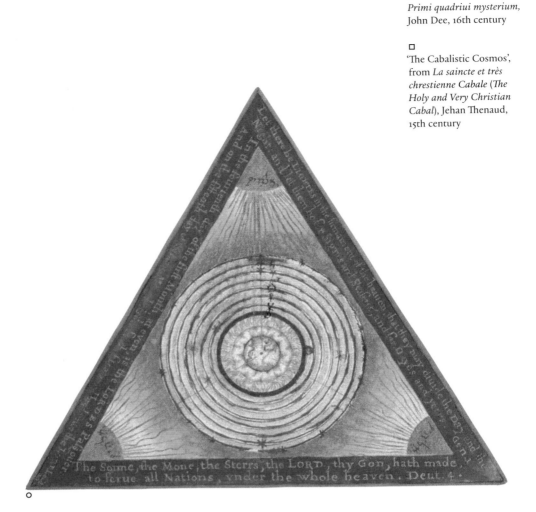

THE SYMBOL OF THE TRIANGLE can be found in many
hermetic cultural traditions, including ancient Egyptian and
Greek, Hinduism and the occult. It may represent the trinity
within humanity of mind, body and spirit (or soul), or the
ideas of creation, preservation and destruction. It can also
be understood as a doorway to spiritual understanding. The
macrocosm of the universe is often depicted with concentric
circles representing spiritual worlds with the Earth at the centre.

'Yggdrasill: The Mundane Tree', illustration by Oluf Olufsen Bagge, from an English translation of the *Prose Edda*, 1847

gold mirrored an inner process of purification and redemption. Jābir ibn Hayyān, purported to have lived in the 8th century and to have authored a vast number of alchemical works, assigned pairings of the basic qualities of hotness, coldness, dryness and moistness to each classical element, holding that by rearranging the qualities of one metal, a different metal could be made. In Europe, during the Renaissance, medical and occult branches of alchemy developed simultaneously with John Dee claiming that the philosopher's stone might be used to communicate with angels. By the 19th century alchemy was considered a mystical practice, rather than a practical science, concerned primarily with achieving spiritual enlightenment.

The ancient symbol of the *axis mundi* (world axis or centre of the world), often represented by the motif of the world tree, extends the concept of the macrocosm being reflected in the microcosm with the idea of an axis, or path, that connects every part of the universe. In depictions of the world tree, the trunk connects the surface of the Earth with the heavens above via its branches and the underworld below via its roots. The world tree in Norse mythology is the ash tree Yggdrasil. It represents the centre of the cosmos and is said to be the place the gods assemble daily to hold their courts. A squirrel, Ratotoskr, runs up and down the trunk, carrying messages between the eagle, who resides at the top of the tree, and the serpent, who lives beneath its roots.

The human body can also be used as a symbol of the world axis, or centre. In *Vitruvian Man* (c. 1492) Leonardo da Vinci (1452–1519) highlights the symmetry and proportion found within the male body, believing that it is a reflection of the design of the universe. In many philosophical traditions around the world, it is believed that individuals might ascend or descend the axis, or path, in pursuit of knowledge and insights from the higher or lower realms with the ultimate aim of moving beyond the microcosmic realm into the macrocosmic. Central to the religious practice of shamanism, originating in north Asia and associated with indigenous and tribal societies, is the belief that a practitioner can journey to the spirit world, perhaps employing trance, to communicate with the spirits and use spiritual energy to heal those in the physical world below. For the Yoruba people of West

YGGDRASILL,

The Mundane Tree

'Tree of Knowledge of Good and Evil',
from *Geheime Figuren der Rosenkreuzer*
(*Secret Symbols of the Rosicrucians*), 1785

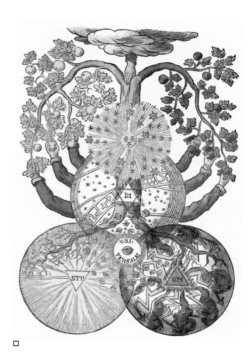

Africa it is the priests known as *babalawos* who provide a link between the spiritual world of *orun*, reigned over by the creator god, Olodumare, and inhabited by lesser deities, or *orisha*, and the material world of *aye*, inhabited by all life on Earth. Using the divinatory system known as *Ifá*, *babalawos* interpret messages from the *orisha* for individuals seeking personal guidance.

The motif of the tree of life is found in many religions, including Christianity. In the Bible, in the Book of Genesis, it is said to be found in the Garden of Eden, where it symbolizes eternal life, alongside the tree of knowledge. The Islamic tree of life described in the Quran is known as the tree of immortality. This tree was traditionally depicted on prayer mats and elaborately carved into the stone windows of mosques, the most famous of which is the Sidi Saiyed mosque (1572–73) in Gujarat, India. The motif often features in palampores – hangings created in the Mughal and Deccan courts during the 18th century. These hand-painted textiles are highly elaborate and intricate in their design, featuring abundant leaves, flowers, fruit and exotic birds around undulating branches and trunk, while many animals cavort around the base of the tree, which is generally depicted growing out of a stylized mound or hill. Mosques often feature floral patterns or depictions of fruit and vegetables in their architecture, alluding to the paradise to be found after death.

The 12th and 13th centuries witnessed the emergence of Jewish Kabbalah – an esoteric mystical teaching of the relationship between the eternal *Ein Sof* (no end) and his creation, the universe. During the Renaissance, it caught the attention of Pico della Mirandola (1463–1494), who developed a form of Christian Kabbalah,

on which Johannes Reuchlin (1455–1522) wrote the text *De arte cabbalistica* (1517). It was Reuchlin who designed the first diagram of the Kabbalistic tree of life. The diagram presents 10 numbered nodes, or spheres, called *sephiroth*, each representing a divine energy, and together depicting the map of creation and humanity's place in it, set out in three columns, or pillars, of energy and interconnected by 22 paths. Rabbi Isaac Luria (1534–1572), known as Arizal, formulated the Kabbalah into a comprehensive system, known as Lurianic Kabbalah, which he taught in Safed, Israel. His disciple Rabbi Hayyim Vital collected all his lecture notes and eventually the *Etz Chaim* [Tree of Life] was produced from them. The Kaballist seeks

THE FOUR ELEMENTS – air, fire, water and earth – were proposed to explain the material basis of the physical universe by ancient Greek philosopher Empedocles (*c.* 494–*c.* 434 BCE), who called them 'roots'. Plato (428/427–348/347 BCE) associated each of the elements with a solid, and Aristotle (384–322 BCE) related each element to pairings of four qualities: air is hot and wet, fire is hot and dry, water is cold and wet, and earth is cold and dry. Alchemist Jābir ibn Hayyān (purported to have lived between 721 and 815 CE) theorized that if metals were composed of a *jawhar* (substance) and two qualities, or *ṭabāʾiʿ* (natures), then by rearranging the *ṭabāʾiʿ* you could transform one metal into another.

○
Illustration of four elements from *L'Ovide moralisé* (Ovid's *Metamorphoses*), French translation, Bruges, 1470–80

□
Illustrations from *Livre des propriétés des choses* (*On the Properties of Things*), Bartholomew the Englishman, translated by Jean Corbechon, 1485

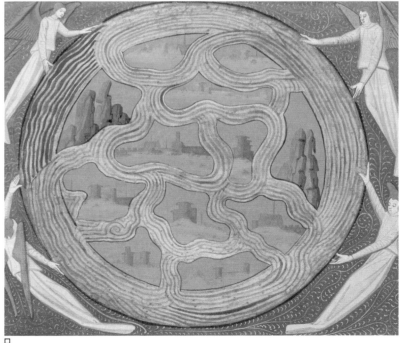

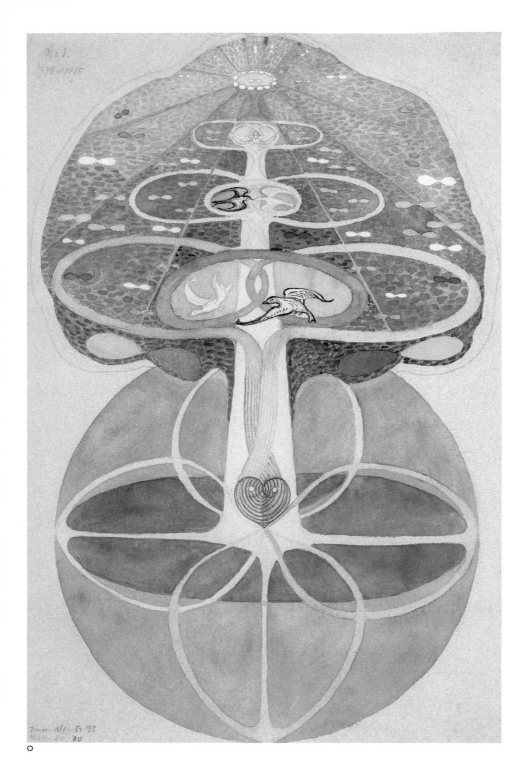

The Cosmic Dance

'Here grows the cure of all, this fruit divine,
Fair to the eye, inviting to the taste,
Of virtue to make wise: what hinders then
To reach, and feed at once both body and mind?'

John Milton, *Paradise Lost*, BOOK IX, 1667

○
Tree of Knowledge, No. 1,
Hilma af Klint, 1913–15

□
The Fall of Man,
Hugo van der Goes,
after 1479

□

'Sapta Chakra', illustration of the parts of the body associated with Kundalini yoga, from a manuscript on the practice of yoga, 1800

self-knowledge and understanding of the universe and God, by ascending the tree of life, sphere by sphere, until he reaches his higher self and spiritual enlightenment.

The wheel of life, or the *Bhavachakra*, represents the Buddhist view of existence as a cycle of life, death and rebirth, which Buddhists seek to escape by achieving enlightenment. The wheel is divided into five or six realms – gods and angry gods, humans, hungry ghosts, animals and hell. The figure depicted holding the wheel is Yama, signifying impermanence, and at the centre of the wheel are the three fires of suffering – greed, ignorance and hatred, represented by a rooster, a pig and a snake. The Buddha generally sits outside the wheel: he has escaped the cycle of life and death.

Multiple circles, or wheels, are central to the concept of the *chakras*, found in early Hindu, Buddhist and Jainist traditions. By the early medieval period *chakras* had come to symbolize nodes of psychic energy within the physical body, every human being existing simultaneously on a physical level and a psychological and mental level, known as the 'subtle body'. The two planes affect one another, so if one is damaged or blocked the other will suffer corresponding harm. The number of key *chakras* in the body varies between four and seven, depending on precise belief. Each node is arranged in a column from the base of the spinal cord to the crown of the head, connected by vertical pathways called *nadi*. By energizing each *chakra* through breathing exercises, meditations and mantras, energy flow through the *chakras* remains fluid, and mind and body maintain an even balance. In Tantric thinking, by bringing each *chakra* into alignment, the practitioner can achieve perfect harmony of mind, body and spirit, and thereby attain full spiritual understanding or awakening.

Meditation plays a key part in Hinduism, Buddhism, Jainism and Shintoism, and mandalas and associated mantras aid the individual in its practice. The geometric composition of a mandala usually features representations of deities, paradises and shrines, forming a spiritual map for the practitioner, who journeys from the outermost ring to the centre, contemplating the content of each layer in turn. In a simple Hindu mandala a deity is depicted in a circle in the centre of a square with a gate on each side in the shape of a 'T'. A Buddhist mandala might depict the Pure Land or it might visualize the entire universe with Mount Meru as the *axis mundi*

◻
A Tibetan 'Five Deity Mandala' with Rakta Yamari
(the Red Enemy of Death) embracing his consort,
Vajra Vetali, in the centre, 17th century

◻

in the centre, or it might present the five Buddhas, each embodying a different aspect of enlightenment. Common symbols include a wheel with eight spokes, representing the perfect universe and the Eightfold Path to Enlightenment of Buddhism, a ring of fire, symbolizing the purification of wisdom, a ring of eight tombs, reminding the practitioner of the impermanence of life, and the lotus flower, indicating balance through symmetry and representing in its growth from under water towards the light, the desire to reach for spiritual enlightenment. Mandala designs can be found in many Buddhist temples and stupas, including at Borobudur, the 7th-century Buddhist temple in Java. Sand mandalas are made by Tibetan Buddhists and are then quickly destroyed to illustrate impermanence.

Sandpainting is a crucial part of the healing ceremonies practised by the Navajo people of southwestern USA. The sandpaintings are based on traditional symmetrical Navajo designs, featuring images of holy people. Each sandpainting acts as a portal to the spirit world. The medicine man or woman calls on the spirits of the holy people depicted in the sandpainting to enter the design while the patient sits on top of it to absorb the spiritual power and allow the spirits to ingest the illness. At the end of the ceremony the sandpainting is destroyed and with it the illness it has absorbed.

In its geometric presentation of symbols, the Aztec Sun Stone is a form of mandala. Carved by the Aztecs during the reign of Moctezuma II, between 1501 and 1520, it was discovered in 1790 under the main square of Mexico City, previously the Aztec capital of Tenochtitlan. At the centre of the vast, intricately carved stone is what is thought to be the face of the solar deity Tonatiuh. Around the central deity are carved four squares representing the four previous suns or eras. These are surrounded by a concentric circle of signs corresponding to the 20 days of the Aztec calendar. It is likely that the Sun Stone was used in sacred rituals, involving human heart sacrifice, conducted to ensure the Earth's survival for the next Aztec cycle of 52 years.

The creation of imagery has always been integral to the development of philosophy and science, religion and the occult. These captivating pages take you on a visual journey from the microcosm to the macrocosm, from the infinitesimal wonders of the subatomic world to the inconceivable vastness of infinite space. Drawn from 3,000 years of philosophical, religious and scientific enquiry, they inspire awe and wonder, impart meaning and promote mindful reflection on the complexity, pattern and beauty of the natural world and the place and purpose of humanity in the universe.

○

○
Illustration of the universe from the
Scivias, Hildegard von Bingen, *c.* 1165

□
'I. Figure Cosmique', woodcut illustration
from *Le Vray et methodique cours de la
physique resolutive: vulgairement dite
chymie*, Annibal Barlet, 1657

'You never enjoy the world aright, till the Sea itself
floweth in your veins, till you are clothed with the
heavens, and crowned with the stars: and perceive
yourself to be the sole heir of the whole world, and
more than so, because men are in it who are every
one sole heirs as well as you.'

Thomas Traherne, quoted in *Centuries of Meditations*, 1908

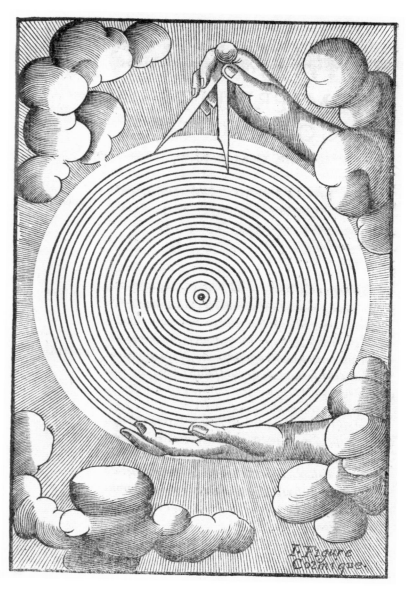

○
A paper kakemono (hanging scroll) painted in
ink with an ensō (circle), by Mugaku, formerly
at the Daitokuji temple, 18th century

□
Japan First Zen Cave (monastery),
Sengai Gibon, 1819–28

*'In my hut this spring,
There is nothing –
There is everything!'*

Yamaguchi Sodo, from *Haiku*, VOL. II, 1950,
translated by R. H. Blyth

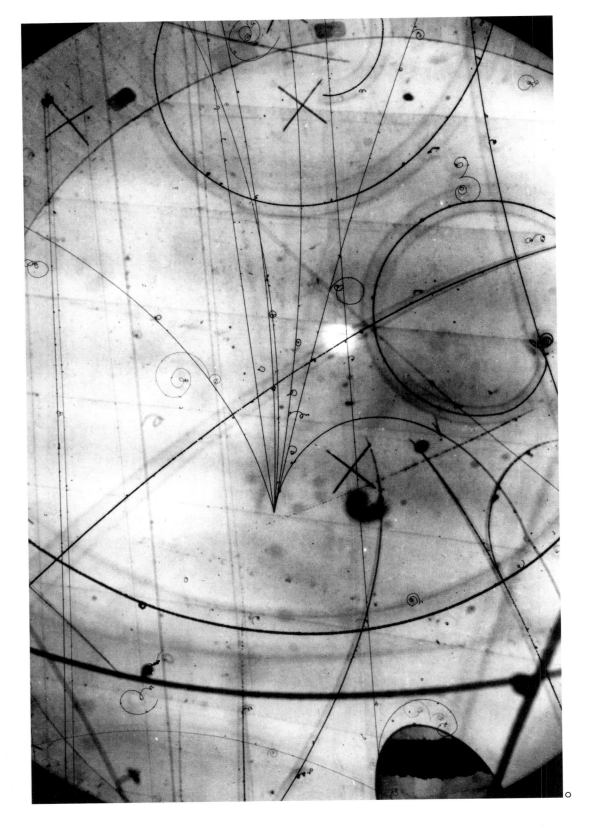

1. The Infinitesimal Universe

*'To see a World
in a Grain of Sand
And a Heaven
in a Wild Flower
Hold Infinity in the
palm of your hand
And Eternity in an hour.'* ᐃ

○
Tracks made by atomic particles from
a particle accelerator, Fermi National
Accelerator Laboratory, Batavia,
Illinois, USA, 1978

ᐃ
William Blake,
'Auguries of Innocence', 1863

It was not until the invention of the microscope that natural scientists could begin to study in detail the anatomy of plants or the design of living organisms, firstly at cellular and later at molecular level. From the 17th to the 19th centuries their beautiful and forensically detailed drawings of algae, insects, plants and animals, as seen through lenses of ever greater magnifying power, improved humanity's understanding of the marvellous and complex structures of the plant, animal and mineral kingdoms, and later informed the germ theory of disease and epidemiology. Observing natural materials under the microscope – from diatoms to butterfly wings and from capillaries to snowflakes – revealed intricate and beautiful patterns and forms that influenced the work of artists as well as scientists.

In London in 1621 Dutch inventor Cornelis Drebbel (1572–1633) publicly presented a compound microscope with a convex objective lens and a convex eyepiece. Galileo Galilei (1564–1642) saw and improved on this design and in 1624 presented his *occhiolino* ('little eye') to Prince Federico Cesi (1585–1630), founder of the Accademia dei Lincei in Rome. Secretary to the academy, Giovanni Faber, dubbed it a 'microscope', derived from the Greek *micron*, meaning 'small', and *skopein*, meaning 'to look at'. The following year Francesco Stelluti (1577–1652) and Federico Cesi published the broadsheet *Apiarium*. The first publication to include observations made with a microscope, it featured drawings of the anatomy of a bee as seen through a microscope at 10 times magnification, alongside text about the nature and symbolism of bees and descriptions of varieties of bees.

Formed in 1660, The Royal Society appointed polymath Robert Hooke (1635–1703) Curator of Experiments in 1663. Two years later it published Hooke's influential *Micrographia* – the first book to include drawings of insects and plants as seen through microscopes. Hooke created his meticulously detailed drawings from multiple observations of similar specimens at different angles, using lenses of varying strengths. He was the first to use the term 'cell' in a biological sense and observed that plant cells were walled like the cells of a honeycomb. The Royal Society went on to publish biologist and physician Marcello Malpighi's (1628–1694) works depicting specimens as seen through a microsope in 1675 and 1679. Malpighi was the first to see the capillary structures in a frog's lungs and to notice the small holes, or tracheae, in the skin of invertebrates through which they breathe, and he was one of the earliest to observe red blood cells. A talented artist, he made exquisite and detailed drawings of the individual organs of flowers and investigated the lifecycle of plants and animals. The 'Father of Microbiology'

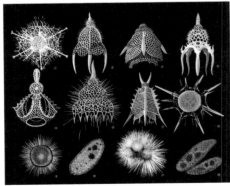

o

Antonie van Leeuwenhoek (1632–1723) was the first to observe microbes through single-lensed microscopes of his own design and making, capable of magnification up to 275 times. In letters to The Royal Society in 1676 he described and depicted unicellular organisms, including bacteria and protozoa.

Zoologist and naturalist Ernst Haeckel (1834–1919) made more than 100 detailed colour illustrations of animals and sea creatures – many first described by Haeckel himself – which were published in *Kunstformen der Natur* between 1899 and 1904. In the display of the individual specimens on each plate Haeckel attempted to convey the symmetry inherent in the different species to reflect his belief in the theory of the evolutionary development of non-random form. Scottish biologist and mathematician, D'Arcy Wentworth Thompson (1860–1948), was also a believer in symmetry and pattern in the forms of animals and plants. In his 1917 work *On Growth and Form*, he argued that the form and structure of living organisms were determined by physical laws and mechanics.

Physicist and musician Ernst Chladni (1756–1827) was the first to demonstrate that the vibrations caused by sound create distinct patterns, depending on the frequency of the sound waves produced. He covered a piece of metal with sand and drew the bow of a violin over it. The sand settled along nodal lines where the surface was still, creating a simple vibration pattern, now known as a Chladni figure. His findings were published in his book *Entdeckungen über die Theorie des Klanges* (1787).

The development of photography in the second half of the 19th century provided scientists and artists with new ways of capturing

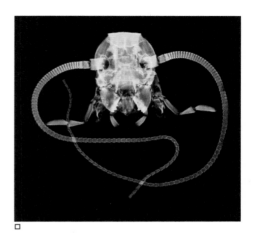
□

and presenting the natural world. In 1885 meteorologist Wilson Bentley (1865–1931) combined a compound microscope with a bellows camera to photograph snowflakes one by one in sub-zero temperatures in Vermont, USA. Transferring each one carefully from a piece of black card to a microscopic slide, he captured more than 5,000 images of snow crystals in his lifetime, describing them as 'ice flowers'. Astronomer Étienne Léopold Trouvelot (1827–1895) married art and science through his exposure of brief bursts of electrical energy to photosensitive plates to create spontaneous abstract images, resembling branching coils, coral or neurons, each fixed permanently in a unique pattern, known as a Trouvelot figure. Similar branching patterns, known as Lichtenberg figures, can be made by discharging high voltage electricity onto the surface of an insulator and then sprinkling a coloured powder over it. The powder adheres to the stranded areas of charge, revealing delicate radial patterns.

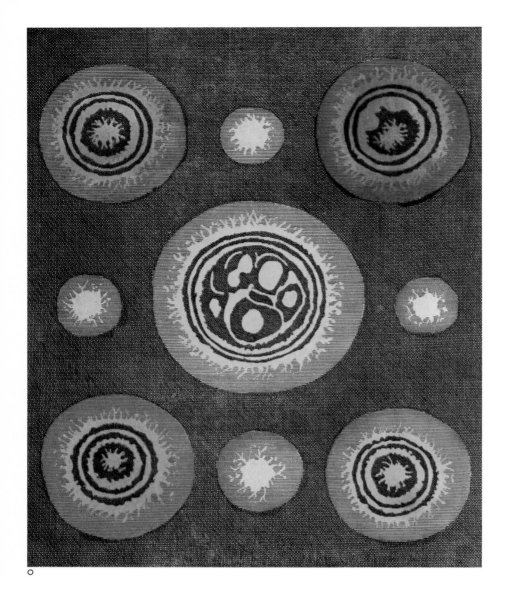

○
'Electrical Stars', copper plate illustration
from *A Key to Physic, and the Occult Sciences*,
Ebenezer Sibly, 1792

□
Woman and model of a dense atomic cloud,
J. P. Wolff, *c.* 1950

The Cosmic Dance

EBENEZER SIBLY (1751–*c.* 1799) was a British astrologer and physician, best known for casting a horoscope for the birth of the United States, published in 1787. He was a supporter of Franz Mesmer's (1734–1815) theory of animal magnetism, which held that an invisible magnetic fluid was naturally present in all living things and could affect the health of the organism. In *A Key to Physic, and the Occult Sciences,* Sibly explained how the magnetic fluid in the body can be manipulated by methods used by mesmerists, including the laying on of hands, to produce beneficial physical effects, such as healing.

○
Lichtenberg Figures: A. R. von Hippel, György Kepes, 1951

□
Direct electric spark obtained with a Ruhmkorff coil or Wimshurst machine, also known as a 'Trouvelot figure', Étienne Léopold Trouvelot, 1888

'Then there is electricity, the demon, the angel, the mighty physical power, the all-pervading intelligence! … by means of electricity, the world of matter has become a great nerve, vibrating thousands of miles in a breathless point of time.'

Nathaniel Hawthorn, *The House of Seven Gables*, 1851

○

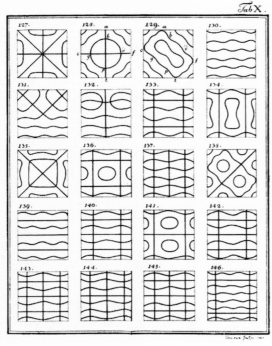

○

'Klangfiguren' (Sound Figures), diagrams from *Entdeckungen über die Theorie des Klanges* (*Discoveries in the Theory of Sound*), Ernst Chladni, 1787

□

Light reflected off tuning forks creates predictable patterns, from *Sound and Music*, John Augustine Zahm, 1892

○

The Cosmic Dance

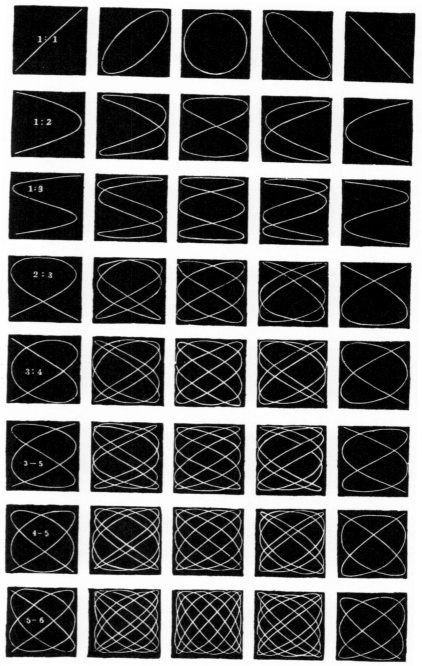

○

○
Untitled Blue Sponge Relief,
Yves Klein, 1960

□
Cover of *Hamonshū,*
Mori Yūzan, 1903

The Cosmic Dance

'To witness, to enter this essence,
this silence, this blue, colour.'

William Heyen, 'Blue' from *The Swastika Poems*, 1977

Crystalized ascorbic acid on a microscope slide in a polarized light by Cosmodernism (Kamil Czapiga), 2021

The Concert, Brazilian agate quartz crystals, Professor Bernardo Cesare, 2021

The Cosmic Dance

'Crystals grew inside rock like arithmetic flowers. They lengthened and spread, added plane to plane in an awed and perfect obedience to an absolute geometry that even stones – maybe only the stones – understood.'

Annie Dillard, *An American Childhood*, 1987

○ Soap bubbles on a microscope slide by
Cosmodernism (Kamil Czapiga), 2021

□ Microphotographs of snowflakes,
Wilson Bentley, *c.* 1890

○

ON 15 JANUARY 1885 WILSON 'SNOWFLAKE' BENTLEY (1865–1931) became the first person to photograph an individual snowflake. A pioneer in photomicrography, Bentley documented more than 5,000 snowflakes over 40 years. A selection of Bentley's photomicrographs were published in *Popular Science Monthly* in May 1898 as part of an article entitled 'A Study of Snow Crystals', which he wrote in collaboration with naturalist George Henry Perkins. They were the first scientists to assert that no two snowflakes are exactly alike.

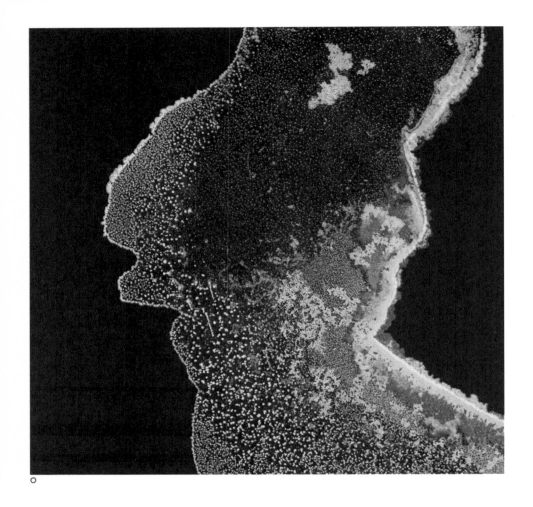

o

'Oh, for Medea's wondrous alchemy,
Which wheresoe'er it fell made the earth gleam
With bright flowers, and the wintry boughs exhale
From vernal blooms fresh fragrance!'

Percy Bysshe Shelley, *Alastor; or, The Spirit of Solitude*, 1816

□

Acide urique du ruminant, a micrograph
of uric acid taken from a ruminant animal,
Laure Albin-Guillot, 1931

□

UNICELLULAR MICROALGAE CALLED DIATOMS are found singly or in colonies in almost every aquatic or moist environment on Earth, and are responsible for 20 to 50 per cent of the oxygen produced each year. Diatoms were first illustrated in 1703, but it was not until 1783 that the first one was formally identified by naturalist Otto Friedrich Müller. Varying in size between 2 and 200 micrometres, diatoms are either centric (radially symmetric) or pennate (bilaterally symmetric) in shape and all have hard, porous cell walls composed mainly of silica. Approximately 16,000 species of diatom have now been identified.

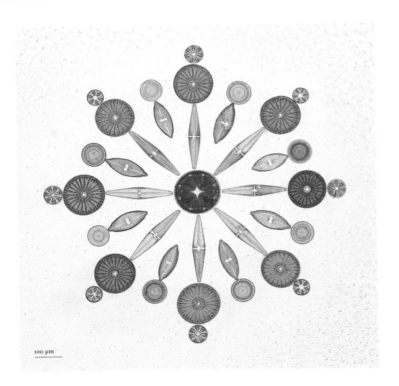

100 μm

○
Arranged diatoms on microscope slides in the California Academy of Sciences Diatom Collection; *above*: photograph of diatoms arranged on a microscope slide by W. M. Grant; *below*: photograph of diatoms collected in Russia and arranged on a microscope slide in 1952 by A. L. Brigger; *scale bar* = 100 μm

□
Darkfield photomicrograph of fossil diatoms, Lomita, California, USA

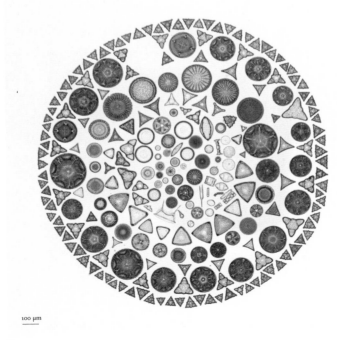

100 μm

○

The Cosmic Dance

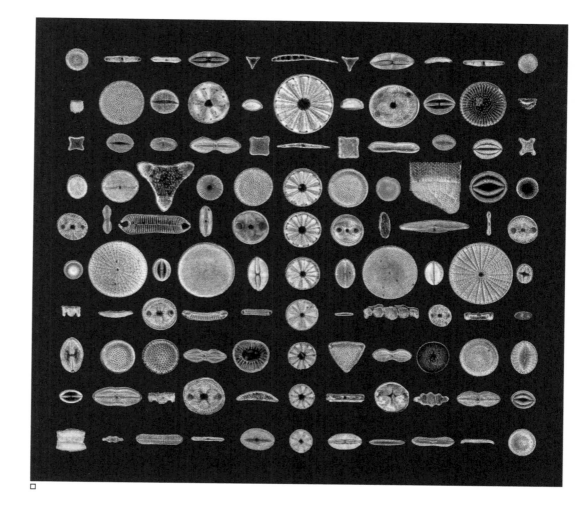

'We cannot fathom the marvellous complexity of an organic being. ... Each living creature must be looked at as a microcosm – a little universe, formed of a host of self-propagating organisms, inconceivably minute and as numerous as the stars in heaven.'

Charles Darwin, *The Variation of Animals and Plants Under Domestication,* 1868

○

The Cosmic Dance

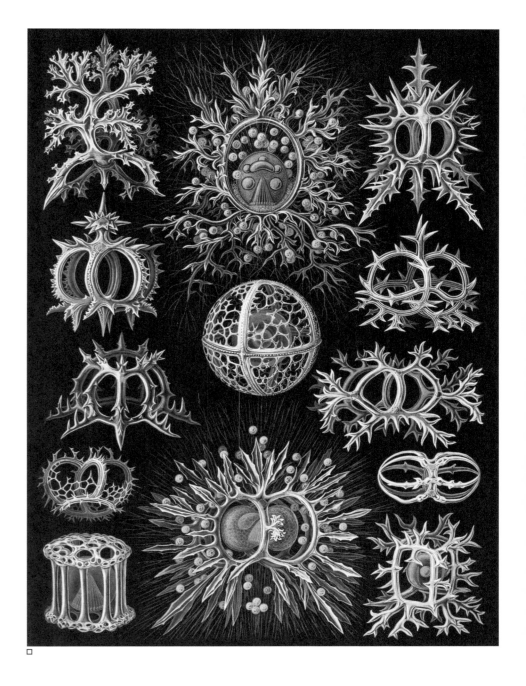

○
'Radiolaria', from *Le Monde de la mer*
(*The World of the Sea*), Alfred Frédol, 1866

□
'Stephoidea', from *Kunstformen der Natur*
(*Art Forms of Nature*), Ernst Haeckel, 1904

○

○ 'Acanthophracta', from *Kunst-*
formen der Natur (*Art Forms*
of Nature), Ernst Haeckel, 1904

□ *Group IV, The Ten Largest, No. 7,*
Adulthood, Hilma af Klint, 1907

The Cosmic Dance

'Where the telescope ends, the microscope begins. Which of the two has the grander view? Choose. A bit of mould is a pleiad of flowers; a nebula is an anthill of stars.'

Victor Hugo, *Les Misérables*, 1862, translated by Charles E. Wilbour

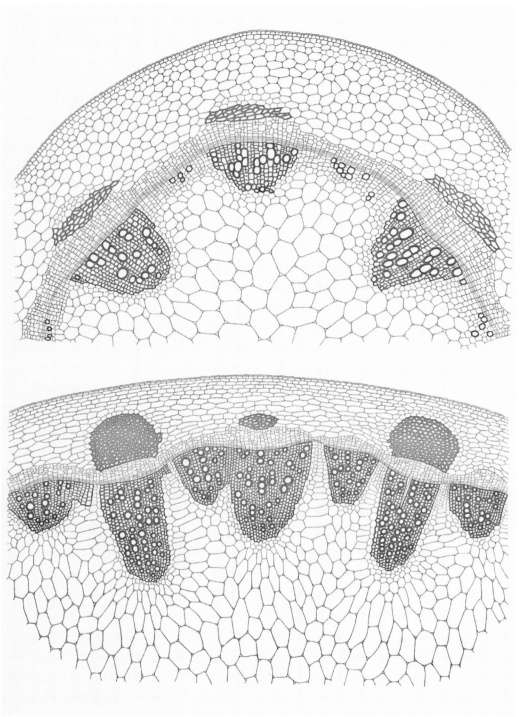

The Cosmic Dance

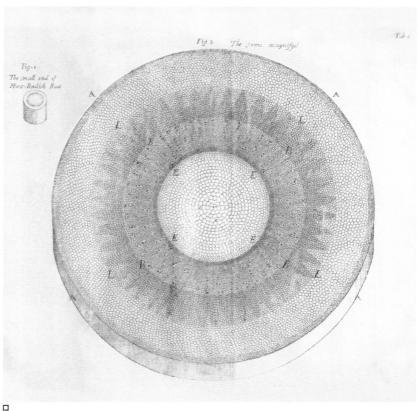

'There is nothing you can see that
is not a flower; there is nothing you
can think that is not the moon.'

Matsuo Bashō, from *Haiku*, VOL. I, 1949,
translated by R. H. Blyth

○
Cross-section of the stem of a
dicotyledon plant from *Anatomia
vegetal* (*Vegetal Anatomy*), Frederik
Elfving, 1929

□
Cross-section of a plant from *Anatomy
of Plants*, Nehemiah Grew, 1680

○

○
Carnival of Onions, gelatin silver
print, Midori Shimoda, early 1930s

□
Throbbing Pulse,
Louise Bourgeois, 1944

The Cosmic Dance

○

Image of a dog's olfactory bulb from *Sulla fina anatomia degli organi centrali del sistema nervoso* (*Anatomy of the Central Organ of the Nervous System*), Camillo Golgi, 1885

□

Development of an egg from *Atlas d'embryologie* (*Atlas of Embryology*), Mathias Duval, 1889

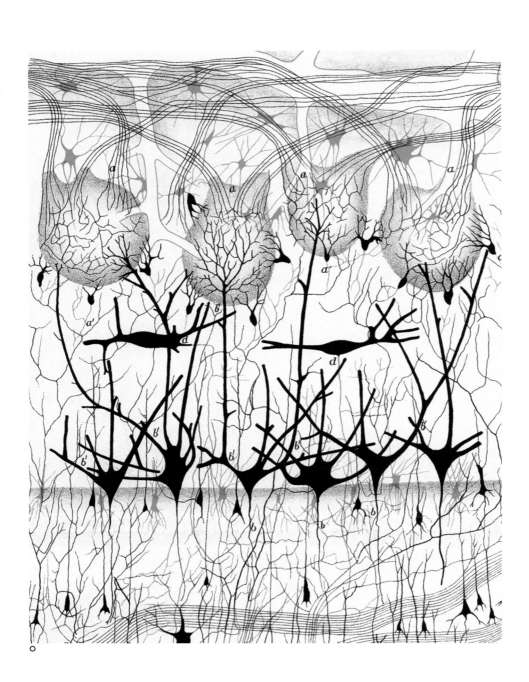

○

'Every bird which flies has the thread of the infinite in its claw. Germination includes the hatching of a meteor and the tap of a swallow's bill breaking the egg, and it leads forward the birth of an earthworm and the advent of Socrates.'

Victor Hugo, *Les Misérables*, 1862, translated by Charles E. Wilbour

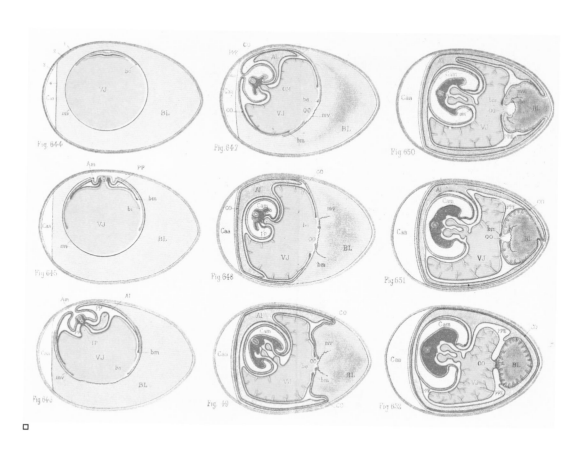

A Purkinje neuron from the human
cerebellum, Santiago Ramón y Cajal, 1899

Untitled, no. 7 of 14, from *À l'Infini* (set 1),
Louise Bourgeois, 2008

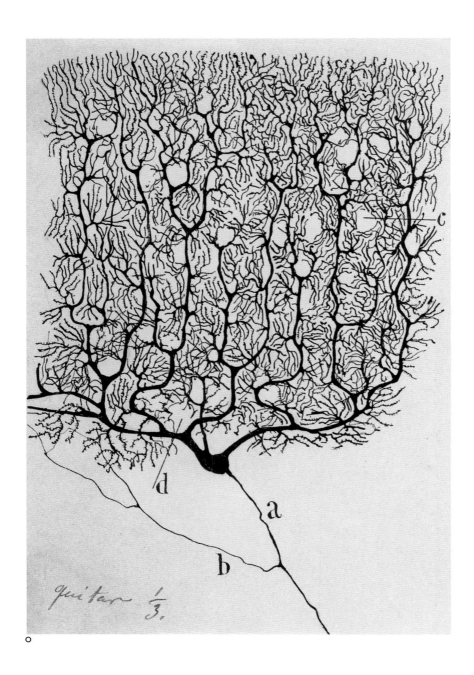

SANTIAGO RAMÓN Y CAJAL (1852–1934) was a pioneer in the investigation of the microscopic structures of the nervous system, in particular of the brain and spinal cord. In 1887, employing the Golgi stain, he observed discrete cells, or neurons, each with multiple branches growing from a cell body and with a long thread-like appendage called an axon, and made detailed drawings of them. He proposed that nerve cells were not part of a continuous single network, as had been previously thought, but rather thousands of individual cells with gaps in between them, known as synapses. In 1906, together with Camillo Golgi, he received the Nobel Prize for Physiology or Medicine for his work, which became the foundation of the neuron doctrine.

'Nothing originates in a spot where there is no sentient, vegetable and rational life; feathers grow upon birds and are changed every year; hairs grow upon animals and are changed every year.'

Leonardo da Vinci, quoted in *The Notebooks of Leonardo da Vinci*, 1970

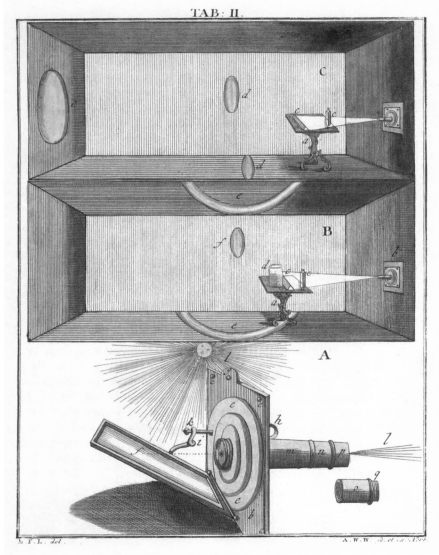

The Cosmic Dance

Illustration of a solar microscope
(plate II), Adam Wolfgang Winterschmidt
after Martin Frobenius Ledermüller, 1768

Illustration of butterfly wing scales
(plate IX), Adam Wolfgang Winterschmidt
after Martin Frobenius Ledermüller, 1766

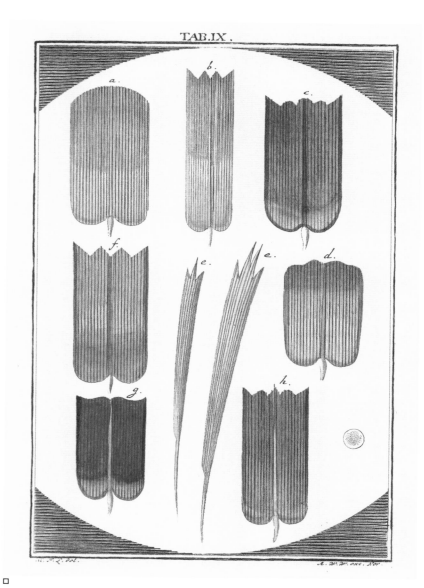

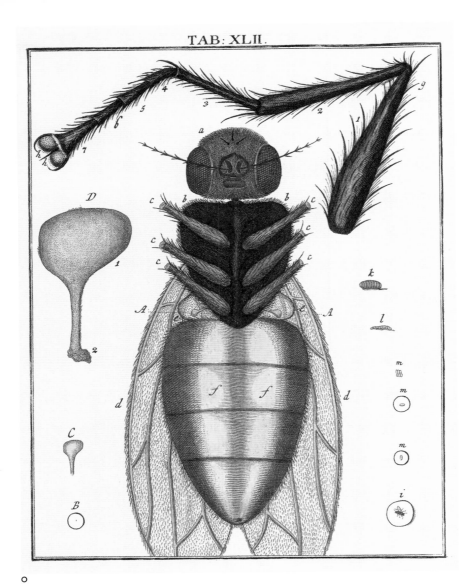

○
Illustration of a fly (plate XLII),
Adam Wolfgang Winterschmidt after
Martin Frobenius Ledermüller, 1768

□
Illustration of a fly (plate XXXVII),
Adam Wolfgang Winterschmidt after
Martin Frobenius Ledermüller, 1768

The Cosmic Dance

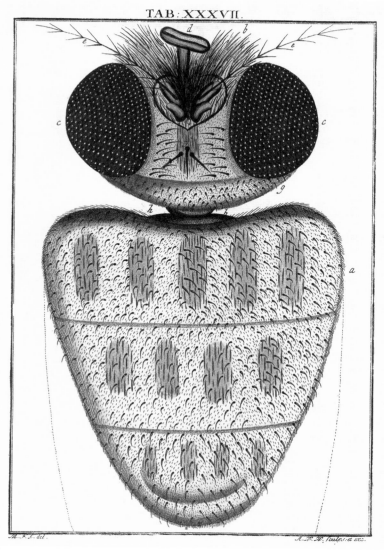

'Nothing is more humbling than to look with a strong magnifying glass at an insect so tiny that the naked eye sees only the barest speck and to discover that nevertheless it is sculpted and articulated and striped with the same care and imagination as a zebra.'

Rudolf Arnheim, *Parables of Sun Light*, 1989

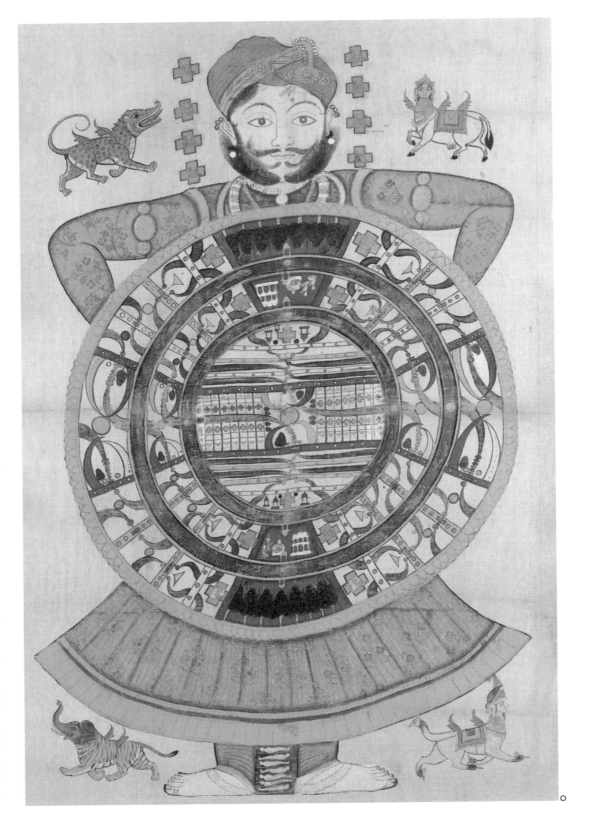

2. God in Miniature

'The skin is like the sky,
the flesh like the earth,
bones like the mountains,
and veins like rivers, blood
in the body like the water
of the sea, a belly like the
ocean, hair like plants,
and breath drawn in
and out as the wind.' △

○
Ink and gouache representation of Loka Purusha, Rajasthan, India, *c.* 1900

△
Bundahishn, a collection of Zoroastrian cosmogony, 1540

According to Chinese mythology every part of the body of the primordial being, or Cosmic Man, Pangu became a particular feature on Earth and in the heavens: his left eye became the sun and his right eye the moon; his bones became mountains and rocks, his flesh the earth and his veins the rivers. In early Vedic texts, Purusha is the cosmic being who created all life. Plato (428/427–348/347 BCE) considered the world to be a living being. In *Timaeus* (*c.* 360 BCE) he argues that the maker of the physical universe is a demiurge or god who 'put intelligence in soul, and soul in body' to make a living and intelligent, ordered whole out of a state of chaos. It created the universe out of the four elements – fire, earth, water and air – in the shape of a globe, the most perfect geometric form. Then it created the soul of the universe and divided the substance amongst the planets. Finally, it connected the body and soul of the universe by placing the soul at its centre and causing it to travel outwards in every direction until every part was suffused with it. Timaeus goes on to explain that the structure of the human body corresponds exactly to that of the entire universe; that it is a *mikros kosmos*, or little world, of the *makros kosmos*, or great world.

The father of Western medicine, Hippocrates (*c.* 460–370 BCE), regarded health and illness as natural phenomena, observing the same natural laws as the rest of the universe. He argued that the human body contained four bodily fluids or humours: black bile, yellow bile, phlegm and blood, which, in a healthy body, are balanced equally. An excess or lack of one or more of these humours might provoke an extreme emotion or mood and it might also make the body more susceptible to a particular kind of disease. If a person became sick, the humours had become unbalanced, perhaps because of environmental factors or a change in diet; the cure was to restore them to perfect balance. Influential Greek physician Galen (129–*c.* 216 CE) developed the theory further, linking the four humours to personality type. Where one humour dominated, the temperament of the individual would reflect the qualities of that humour: an excess of black bile, for example, would result in a melancholic temperament.

In Hindu and Buddhist tradition, a strong connection between the physical body and the mental plane, known as the 'subtle body', is thought to be the key to good health. The subtle body consists of *nadi*, or energy channels, connected by circular nodes called *chakra*, the most important of which are arranged in a line down the spinal column. Through meditation each *chakra* can be energized and the psychic energy between them kept flowing, ensuring that mind and body are kept in perfect balance.

Galen also adopted Plato's theory of
the tripartite soul, outlined in the *Republic*:
logistikon, or reason, located in the head,
thumoeides, or spirit, located in the chest,
and *epithumetikon*, or desire, located in the
stomach. Plato went on to relate each part
of the soul and body to different sections of
society. In Plato's body politic the ruling class
is identified with reason; the warrior class
with spirit; and the ordinary citizen with
desire. For society (and the individual) to
work harmoniously, the lower sections must
fulfil their key function and obey the higher
sections and the highest section must rule
for the benefit of all. Thomas Hobbes (1588–
1679) developed this concept in *Leviathan*
(1651), arguing that all citizens must subject
themselves to the absolute authority of a
sovereign or government, which must rule
in the best interests of all its citizens.

Mathematician and astrologer Claudius
Ptolemy (*c.* 100–*c.* 170 CE) attributed one of
the four elements to each of the twelve signs
of the zodiac. Roman astrologer Marcus
Manilius (1st century CE) codified the system
further in his epic poem *Astronomica*. In
ancient astrology each sign was said to be
governed by three planets, and parts of the
body were linked to astrological signs, working
from the head (Aries) down to the feet (Pisces).
The distribution of the signs was shown in a
diagram known as Zodiac Man. Much later, in
the 14th century, a surgical diagram known as
Wound Man became popular. It illustrated the
injuries that might be inflicted on an individual
through war, disease or accident and offered
a possible cure for each in accompanying text.

Medical astrology and Galen's theories of
the humours and the structure of the human

body were not challenged until the 16th
century when Andreas Vesalius (1514–1564)
published his groundbreaking work on human
anatomy, *De humani corporis fabrica libri septem*
(1543). Based on dissection of the human body,
it presents the body as an integrated structure
framed by its skeletal system and filled with
organs. The book contains detailed anatomical
plates of the body with flaps to lift to examine
the diagram of the organ or muscle beneath
that section of the skin. Vesalius commented
that the human body 'in many respects
corresponds admirably to the universe and
for that reason was called the little universe
by the ancients'.

'Children of the Sun', from
De sphaera, Cristoforo
de Predis, *c.* 1465

Frontispiece from
*Utriusque cosmi,
maioris silicet et minoris,
metaphysica, physica,
atque technica historia*
(*The Giant Cosmos,
Major and Minor,
Metaphysical, Physical
and Technical History*),
Robert Fludd, 1617

PHILOSOPHER AND PARACELSIAN PHYSICIAN ROBERT FLUDD
(1574–1637) believed that divine light acted upon the original dark
chaos to bring about the universe. He held that the divine spirit then
resided in the sun, which conveyed it to the Earth through its rays
to permeate all life. As the sun was to the Earth, so the heart was to
humanity, so the divine spirit was circulated throughout the body
via the blood. In Fludd's view, the spirit could become corrupted
as it moved between macrocosm and microcosm and invade the
microcosm as disease – conceived of as an external invader.

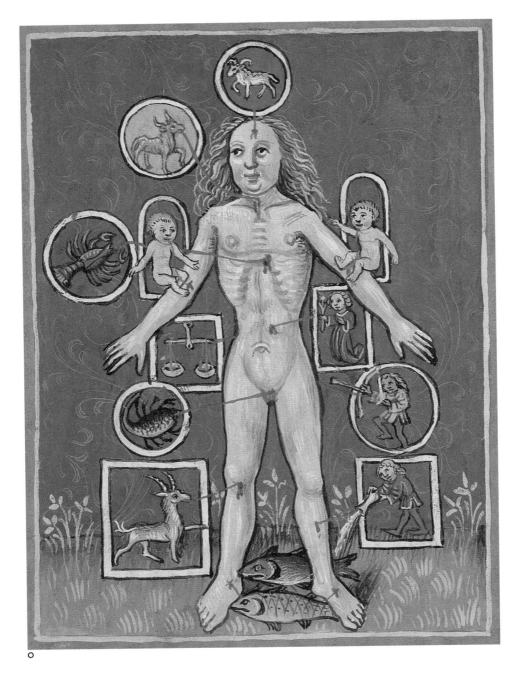

Illustration of Zodiac Man from
Codex Schürstab, Nuremberg,
Germany, *c.* 1472

Illustration of Venus from
Codex Schürstab, Nuremberg,
Germany, *c.* 1472

The Cosmic Dance

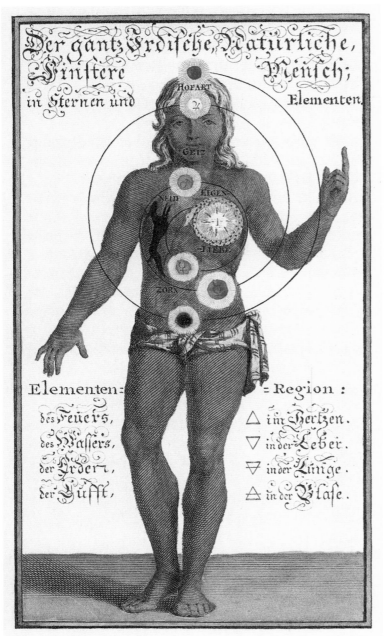

Der gantz Erdische, Natürliche, Finstere Mensch; in Sternen und Elementen.

HOFART

GEIZ

NEID   EIGEN

LIEBE

ZORN

Elementen=
des Feuers,
des Waffers,
der Erden,
der Lufft,

= Region :
△ im Hertzen.
▽ in der Leber.
▽ in der Lunge.
△ in der Blafe.

○

○ 'The Entire Earthly, Natural, and Dark Man', from *Theosophia practica* (*Practical Theosophy*), Johann Georg Gichtel, 1723

□ Painting of Loka Purusha, gouache on cloth, North India, 20th century

THE ARCHETYPAL FIGURE OF COSMIC MAN forms part of the
creation myths of many cultures. According to Chinese legend
the primordial being Pangu created the universe and, after death,
every part of his body became a different physical part of Earth.
In ancient Egypt the creator god Ptah brought the universe
into being with the power of speech. In Indian mythology,
Purusha was conceived of as the cosmic being who created all
life and later was conceived of as the universal principle, eternal,
formless and all-pervading. In the Kabbalah Adam Kadmon is
considered both the divine light of God and the original man.

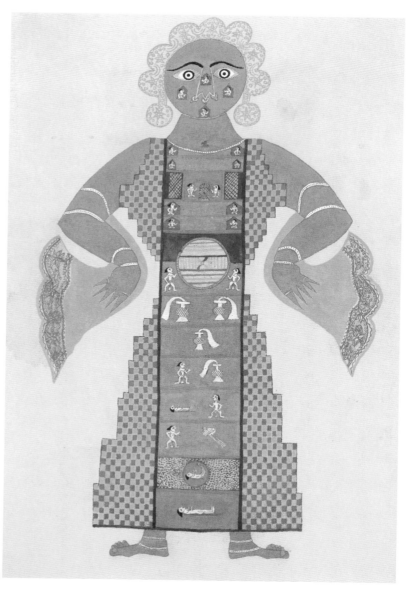

'The pool of blood which lies round the heart is the ocean, and its breathing, and the increase and decrease of the blood in the pulses, is represented in the earth by the flow and ebb of the sea.'

Leonardo da Vinci, quoted in *The Notebooks of Leonardo da Vinci*, 1970

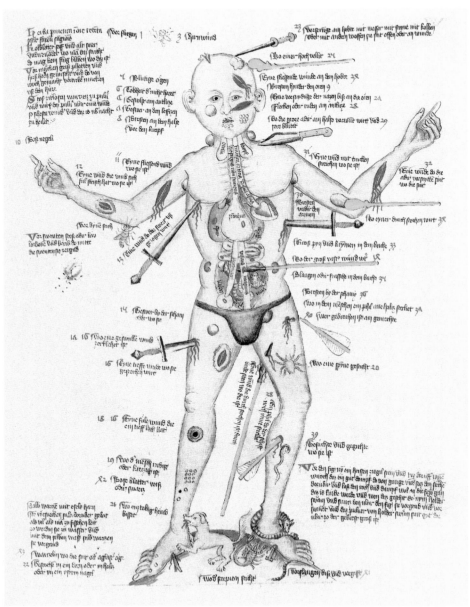

The Cosmic Dance

○
Wound Man diagram and text from
Section III 'Medical and anatomical texts
and drawings' of *The Apocalypse, c.* 1420

□
Illustration of woman with sun, moon
and inner planets from *Grilandas
inventum libri*, Paolo Grillandi, 1506–7

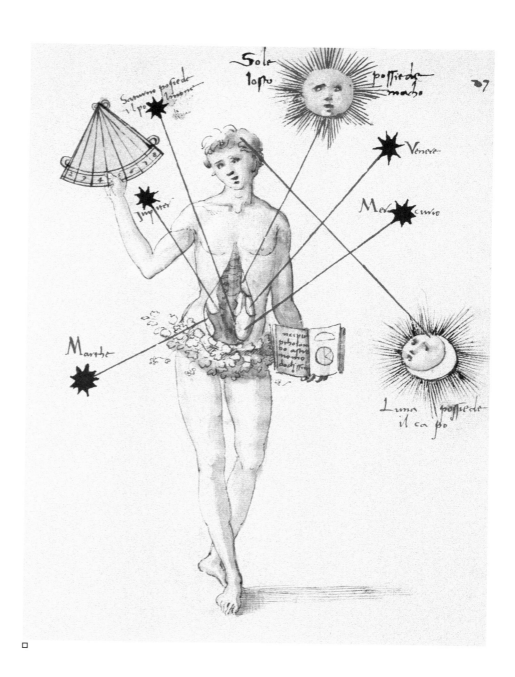

THE HIPPOCRATIC TREATISE *On the Nature of Man* (440–400 BCE) states that the human body contains four humours or fluids – blood, phlegm, yellow bile and black bile, each associated with an organ – blood with the heart, phlegm with the brain, yellow bile with the liver and black bile with the spleen. Greek physician Galen (129–*c.* 216 CE) developed the theory further, attributing to each humour two of the qualities of the four elements – hot or cold with dry or wet. He argued that the four humours might be held in different proportions and strengths within the human body to produce a possible nine different temperaments, the most extreme of which would reflect the names of the four humours themselves: sanguine, phlegmatic, choleric and melancholic.

○
Illustration of the four humours
from *The Guildbook of the Barber
Surgeons of York*, 1486

☐
Fire, oil on wood,
Giuseppe Arcimboldo, 1566

God in Miniature

○
Yantra depicting Mahākāla,
pigments on cloth canopy,
18th–19th century

□
Diagrams of Newar yogic
six-*chakra* transformation,
Nepal, *c.* 1850

The Cosmic Dance

THE WORD *CHAKRA* first appears in Hindu Vedic texts (*c.* 1300–900 BCE) as part of the word *chakravartin*, meaning 'the wheel-turning king'. However, it is not until the 8th century CE that the word *chakra* can be found in Hindu and Buddhist texts in reference to vital energy centres situated along energy channels, or *nadi*, of the 'subtle body' – the non-physical psyche or mind plane. Typically, there were thought to be four to seven key *chakras* arranged in a column from the base of the spinal cord to the crown of the head. However, according to some Hindu traditions, there are many thousands of *chakras* located throughout the multiple *nadi* of the 'subtle body'.

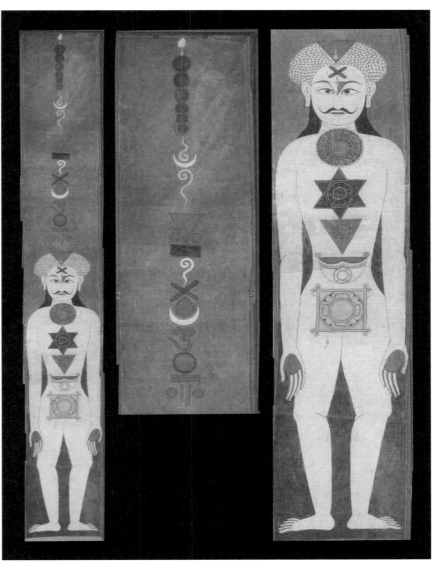

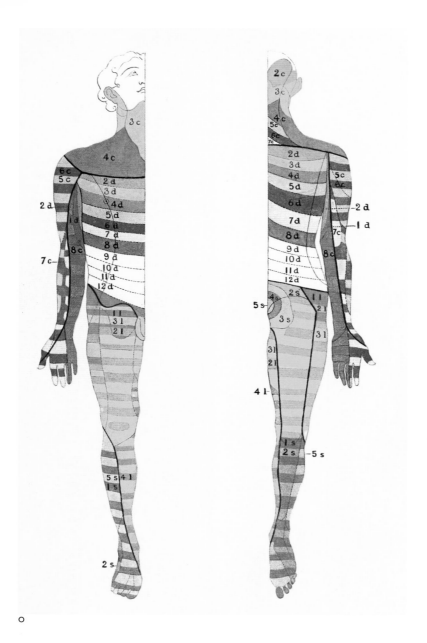

○

○
Illustration from *A Practical Treatise on Medical Diagnosis for Students and Physicians*, John Herr Musser, 1904

□
'Human Aura on F Sharp' from *Psycho-Harmonial Philosophy*, Peter Pearson, 1910

The Cosmic Dance

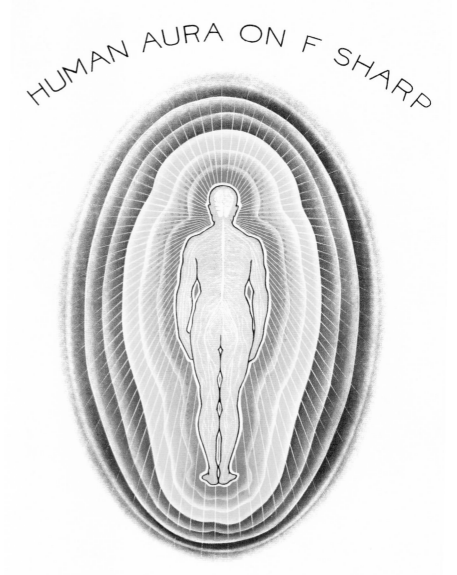

HUMAN AURA ON F SHARP

IN A PERFECT HUMAN BEING ON F SHARP THE PRISMATIC
COLORS IN THE AURA HAVE THE SAME POSITION
AS THEY HAVE IN THE RAINBOW

○

○
Kantha (embroidered quilt) detail,
recycled cotton with cotton embroidery,
undivided Bengal, c. 1900

□
Dance headdress, Sulka people, New
Britain, Papua New Guinea, c. 1880

The Cosmic Dance

'The dance of Shiva is the dancing universe, the ceaseless flow of energy going through an infinite variety of patterns that melt into one another.'

Fritjof Capra, *The Tao of Physics*, 1975

Inauguration of the Pleasure Dome, featuring
Anaïs Nin as Astarte, Kenneth Anger, 1954

Untitled, coloured pencil and felt pen
on cardboard, Janko Domsic, *c.* 1970

The Cosmic Dance

'The least movement is of importance to all nature.
The entire ocean is affected by a pebble.'

Blaise Pascal, quoted in *Forming an Encyclopædia of Quotations
from Ancient and Modern Authors*, 1894

'I give you the end of a golden string,
Only wind it into a ball:
It will let you in at Heaven's gate,
Built in Jerusalem's wall.'

William Blake, *Jerusalem*, 1815

○
'Awake! Awake Jerusalem!', relief etching
printed in orange with pen and black ink,
watercolour and gold, from *Jerusalem*,
William Blake, 1804–20

□
*The Mughal Emperor Jahangir with
Radiant Gold Halo, Holding a Globe,*
life-size portrait in gouache with gold
on fine cotton, Abu al-Hasan, 1617

God in Miniature

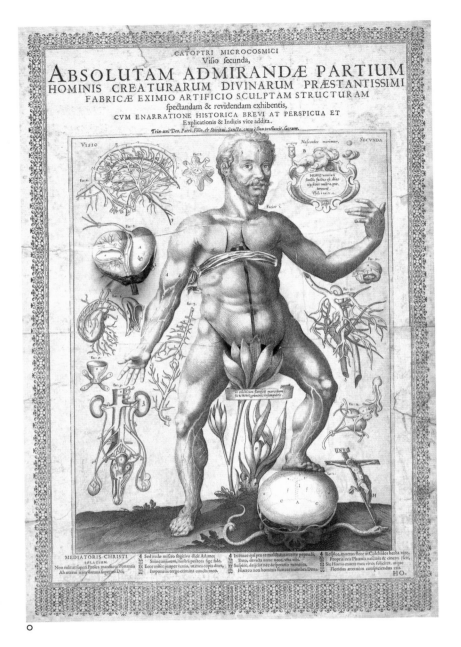

'I profess to learn and to teach anatomy not from books but from dissections, not from the tenets of Philosophers but from the fabric of Nature.'

William Harvey, *The Circulation of the Blood and Other Writings*, 1628

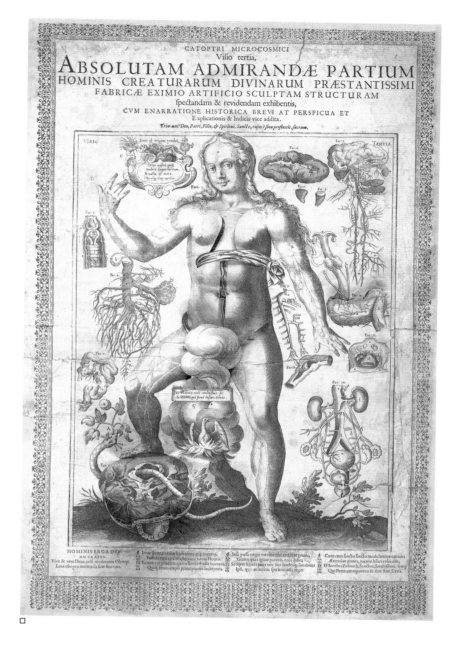

'Second Vision', from *Mirrors of the Microcosm*, Lucas Kilian, 1613

'Third Vision', from *Mirrors of the Microcosm*, Lucas Kilian, 1613

God in Miniature

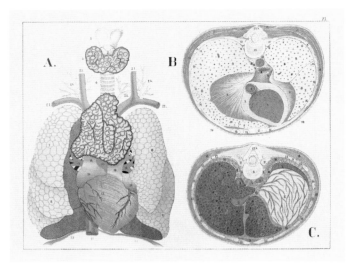

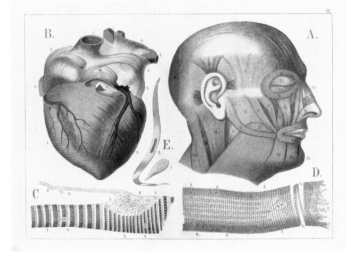

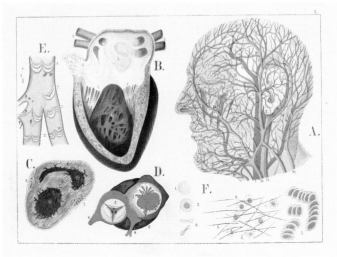

○

Plates from *An Atlas of Anatomy,* Florence Fenwick Miller, 1879

□

Illustration of the circulation of the blood, heart, lungs, arteries and veins from *The Laws of Health,* Joseph C. Hutchison, 1884

○

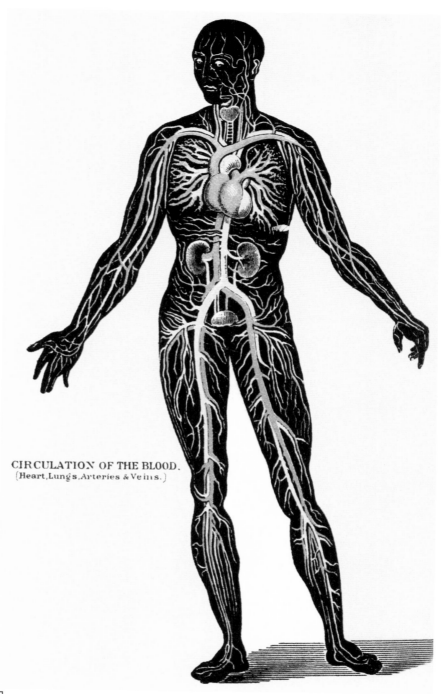

CIRCULATION OF THE BLOOD.
(Heart, Lungs, Arteries & Veins.)

□

God in Miniature

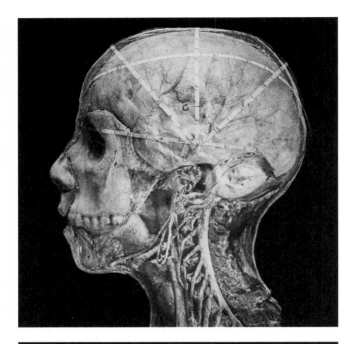

○
Composite photographs
of the human brain from
*A Guide to Operations on
the Brain,* Alec Fraser, 1890

□
A phrenological head divided
into 37 compartments,
O. S. Fowler, *c.* 1840

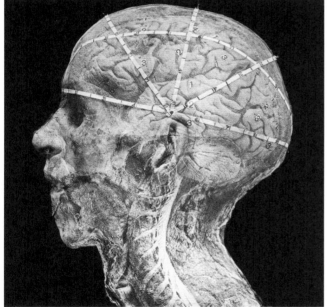

○

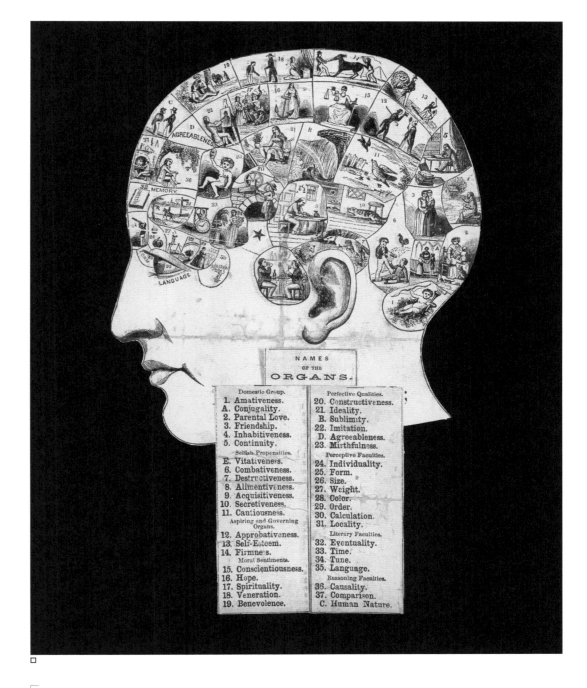

THE PSEUDO-SCIENCE OF PHRENOLOGY was developed by German doctor Franz Joseph Gall (1758–1828). He believed that the human mind features a set of mental faculties, each contained in an organ located in the brain under a specific area of the skull. The larger the area of a particular trait – for example, conscientiousness – the bigger the influence of that trait on the overall personality of the individual concerned.

'[Geometry] is co-eternal with the mind of God. ... Geometry provided God with a model for the Creation and was implanted into man, together with God's own likeness.'

Johannes Kepler, *Harmonices mundi*, 1619

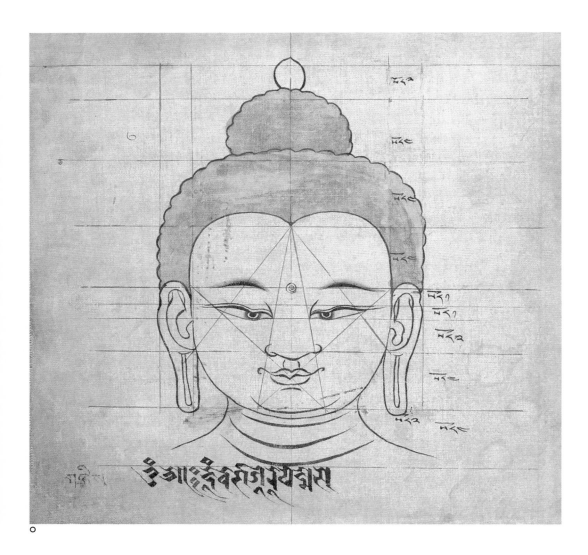

The Cosmic Dance

○
Solomon ceremonial shield,
Santa Isabel Island, Solomon Islands,
c. 1800

□
Mask (*murua*), New Ireland,
Papua New Guinea, *c.* 1890

*'I am dry like a carved image
only my head is God's.'*

Kumalau Tawali, 'The Old Woman's Message',
from *Signs in the Sky*, 1970

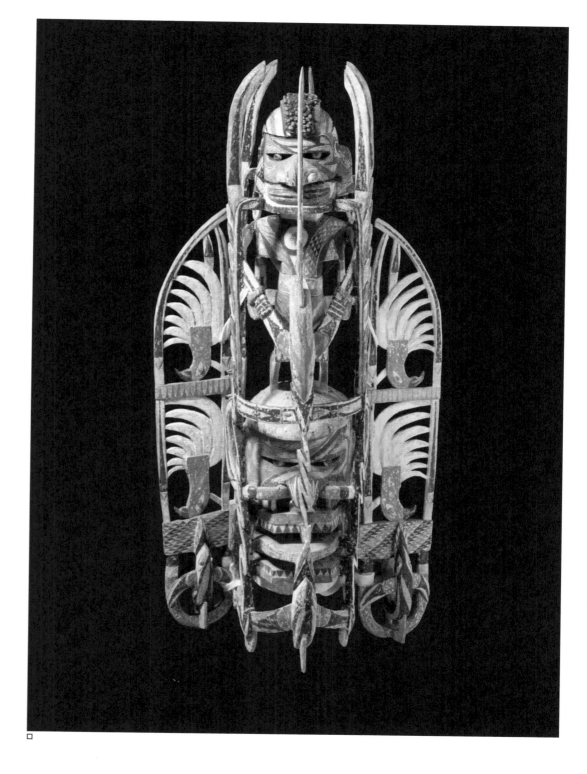

God in Miniature

o

3. Divine Proportions

'*Geometry is one and eternal, shining in the mind of God. That share in it accorded to humans is one of the reasons that humanity is the image of God.*' [△]

○
Acrylic painting by Herbert Bayer to accompany an idea by Alfred North Whitehead (1861–1947): 'The art of progress is to preserve order amid change and to preserve change amid order,' from *Great Ideas of Western Man*, 1964

△
Johannes Kepler, *Harmonices mundi*, 1619

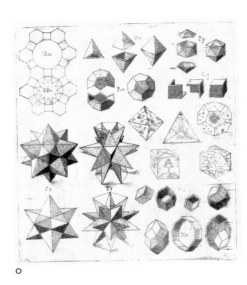
Wen seeking to unlock the secrets of the universe and to explore the correspondences between macrocosm and microcosm, philosophers, scientists and artists have often turned to mathematics. Many have agreed with the astronomer Galileo Galilei (1564–1642), who argued that the 'great book' of the universe is 'written in mathematical language'.

The importance of mathematics to understanding the universe was clear to the ancient Greeks. The Pythagoreans were inspired by their belief that 'all is number'; concepts of harmony, ratio and proportion were central. For Pythagoras (*c.* 570–495 BCE), mathematics formed the basis of the principles of musical harmony, also contained in the mathematical foundations of the universe. He developed the theory of the music, or harmony, of the spheres, proposing that the sun, moon and planets each produced a unique noise based on the speed of their revolution. Together, he held, these sounds made harmonious music which, although imperceptible to the human ear, affected life on Earth. Astronomer Johannes Kepler (1571–1630) developed the theory further in *Harmonices mundi* (1619), making connections between astronomy, music and geometry. He characterized Saturn and Jupiter as basses, Mars as a tenor, Venus and Earth as two altos and Mercury as a soprano. Together they sang in 'perfect accord'. Harmonious music created on Earth was a reflection of the harmonious sounds of the heavens, connecting humanity to the creator of the whole, God.

Plato (428/427–348/347 BCE) believed that five three-dimensional shapes – the Platonic solids – were the basic building blocks of our physical reality. He associated the first of the four shapes with each of the four elements: the cube represented earth, the tetrahedron fire, the icosahedron water and the octahedron air. The fifth shape, the dodecahedron, he associated with the heavens – its twelve faces corresponding to the twelve signs of the zodiac. The dome, first used in tomb architecture of the ancient world, was also associated with the heavens and with perfection in its circular form. During the Renaissance, architect Filippo Brunelleschi (1377–1446) designed and built the most ambitious dome structure since antiquity for Florence Cathedral. It is almost 80 m (262 ft) high and its octagonal base 42 m (138 ft) in diameter – larger than the dome of the Pantheon. Brunelleschi was the first to study linear perspective, laying the groundwork for architect Leon Battista Alberti (1404–1472) who described Brunelleschi's experiments and set out the rules of perspective in *De pictura* (1435).

The harmonious properties of the golden ratio, or golden mean, have been studied since Euclid (*c.* 325–270 BCE). A golden ratio is formed by two sections of a line where the smaller section of the line is in the same ratio to the larger section of the line as the larger section of the line is to the sum of the two sections of the line. A golden rectangle is composed of a square and a smaller rectangle with the same aspect ratio. Artists and architects, including Leonardo da Vinci and Le Corbusier, have used it to create a sense of harmony and proportion in their works. The mathematics underlying God's creation are also revealed by a recurring sequence of numbers originally observed in ancient India. Introduced to the West by mathematician Leonardo of Pisa (*c.* 1170–1250) – later referred to as Fibonacci – in *Liber abaci* (1202), the Fibonacci sequence is one in which each number in a sequence is the sum of the two preceding ones. The ratio between consecutive numbers in the sequence approaches the golden ratio. A golden spiral – a logarithmic spiral in which the growth factor is the golden ratio – also appears in nature, most clearly in the form of the nautilus shell. And examples of natural fractals – a self-similar pattern repeated at ever smaller scale – can be seen in the branching pattern of trees or the leaves of ferns.

Fibonacci's work was a major influence on the mathematician Luca Pacioli (1447–1517), whose *Divina proportione* (1509) examined proportion and its applications to geometry, the visual arts and architecture. Illustrated by Leonardo da Vinci (1452–1519), who called the golden ratio the 'golden section', the treatise connects geometry to understandings of the wider cosmos and God. Physician and natural historian Sir Thomas Browne (1605–1682), exploring the geometry of nature in *The Garden of Cyrus* (1658), identified a recurring pattern known as a quincunx in many natural forms, including the starfish and the wings of flies.

Tessellations – the repeating pattern of geometric shapes containing no overlaps or gaps – have been used to create decorative mosaic tilings since classical antiquity, and are particularly common in Islamic architecture. Only three geometric shapes can form a regular tessellation: an equilateral triangle, a square and a hexagon – as evidenced by the honeycomb in nature. Irregular tessellations, however, can be made by any kind of geometric shape. Artist M. C. Escher (1898–1972), inspired by tessellation he observed in tiling at the Alhambra Palace, Spain, made tessellated patterns out of the interlocking figures of animals. Escher also made so-called impossible drawings, which play with architecture, perspective and mathematical forms to create mind-bending illusions and parallel universes while maintaining a strict internal logic.

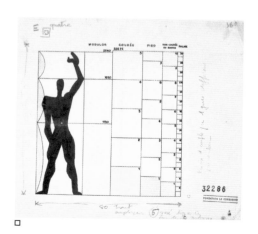

'*I discovered in nature the nonutilitarian delights that I sought in art. Both were a form of magic, both were a game of intricate enchantment and deception.*'

Vladimir Nabokov, 'Butterflies', 1948

222

○
Illustration of fossils from *The Mineral Conchology of Great Britain*, James Sowerby, 1810–45

□
Anatomical drawing of a butterfly, Vladimir Nabokov, 20th century

○

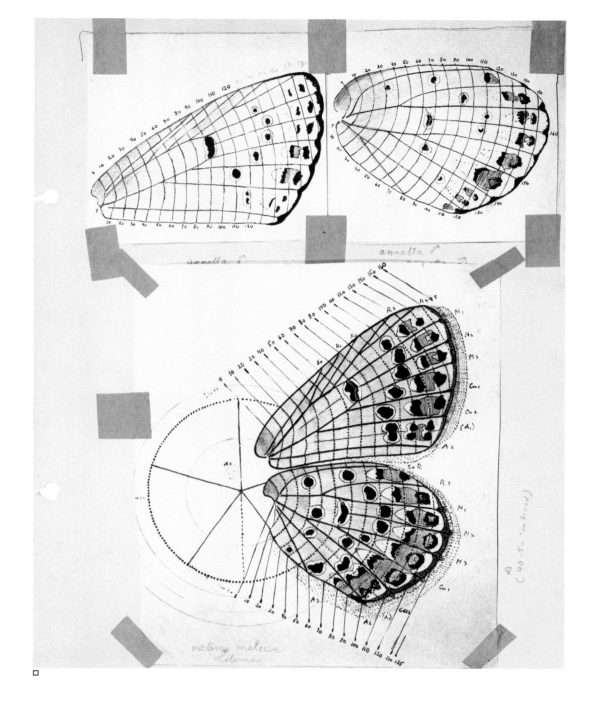

○

'I... have picked up sea shells and
rocks and pieces of wood. ... I have
used these things to say what is
to me the wideness and wonder
of the world as I live in it.'

Georgia O'Keefe, *Some Memories of Drawings*, 1974

○
White Shell with Red,
Georgia O'Keeffe, 1938

□
Radiograph of a Tonnidae
shell, published by Koralle,
1932

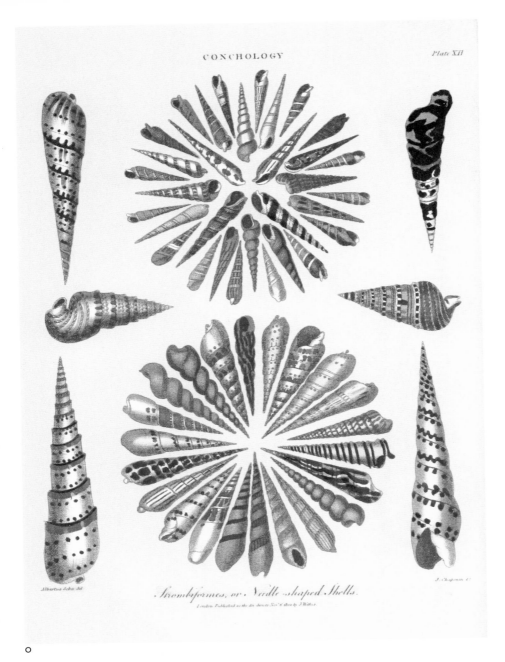

Strombiformes, or Needle-shaped Shells.

Albertus Seba Del.

J. Chapman Sc.

London Published as the Act directs Nov 6 1809 by J Wilkes

Illustration from *Encyclopaedia Londinensis, or, Universal Dictionary of Arts, Sciences, and Literature*, John Wilkes, 1810

Kapkap, an ornament made of clamshell, tortoiseshell, cord and shell beads, Solomon Islands, 19th century

The Cosmic Dance

'E conchis omnia
(*everything from shells*).'

Erasmus Darwin, family motto (from bookplate, 1771)

'How was it not seen that the birth of the
theory of the earth is due to fossils alone.'

Georges Cuvier, *Discours sur les révolutions de la surface du globe* (A Discourse on
the Revolutions of the Surface of the Globe), 1822, translated by Martin J. S. Rudwick

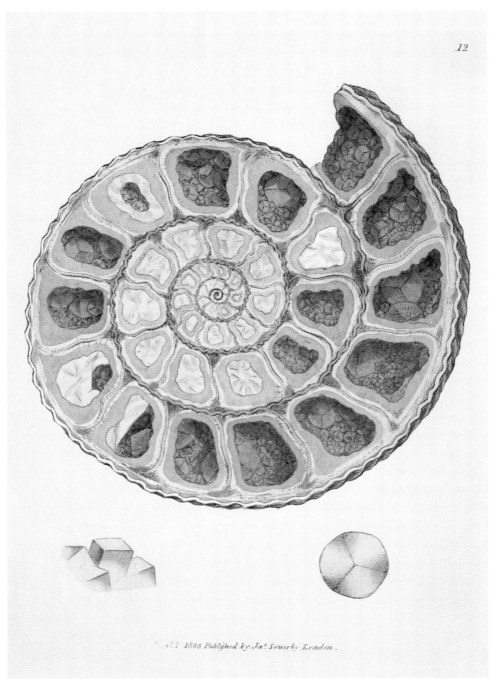

1803 Published by Ja.^s Sowerby London.

○
Illustration from *British Mineralogy:
or Coloured Figures Intended to Elucidate
the Mineralogy of Great Britain,*
James Sowerby, 1804

□
Spiral staircase at Schloss Hartenfels,
Torgau, Germany, designed by
Konrad Krebs, built 1533–37

Divine Proportions

○

○
*A Perspective of a Faceted Snail Shell
Balanced on a Pyramid*, Mathis Zündt,
after Hans Lencker, 1567

□
The Golden Spiral, Marha Plain,
Morocco, by Hannsjörg Voth, 1980–87,
photographed by Ingrid Amslinger

Divine Proportions

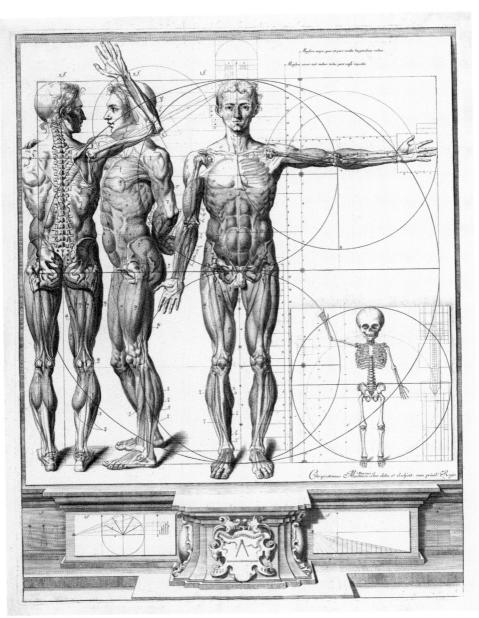

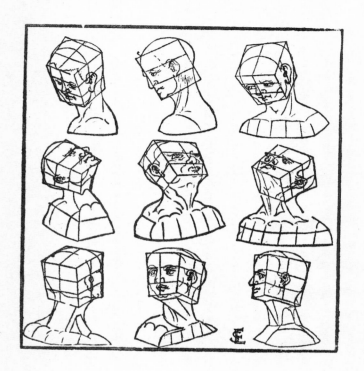

'But can anyone doubt today that all the millions
of individuals and all the innumerable types and
characters constitute an entity, a unit? Though
free to think and act, we are held together, like
the stars in the firmament, with ties inseparable.'

Nikola Tesla, 'The Problem of Increasing Human Energy', 1900

A TIME TABLE

INDICATING THE DIFFERENCE IN TIME BETWEEN THE PRINCIPAL CITIES OF THE WORLD.

WASHINGTON D.C.

AND ALSO SHOWING THEIR AIR-LINE DISTANCE FROM WASHINGTON.

DISTRIBUTION OF COLORS.

N AND S AMERICA
EUROPE
ASIA
AFRICA

DEVICES FOR MEASURING TIME, such as the sundial and water clock, or *clepsydra,* have existed since *c.* 1500 BCE when they were used in ancient Egypt and ancient Babylonia. A sundial is composed of a plate marked out with hour lines and a *gnomon,* or upright blade, which casts a shadow on the plate. As the sun moves across the sky, its shadow moves across the dial, indicating the time of day. The dials were divided into twelve equal segments and operated between sunrise and sunset, meaning that hours were shorter in winter than summer. A water clock works day and night but relies on the provision of a steady flow of water into a container inscribed with measurement lines.

The Cosmic Dance

○
'A Time Table' from *Mitchell's New General Atlas,* Samuel Augustus Mitchell Jr, 1863

□
'A Sundial in the Shape of a Bowl' from *Ars magna lucis et umbrae* (*The Great Art of Light and Shadow*), Athanasius Kircher, 1646

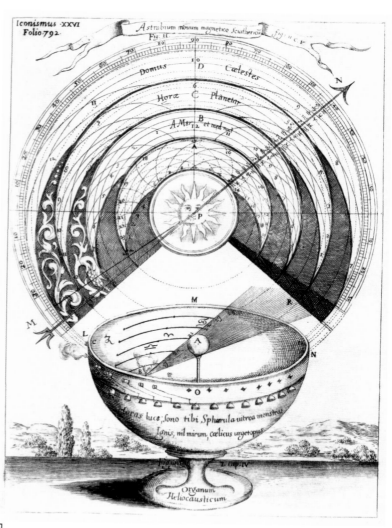

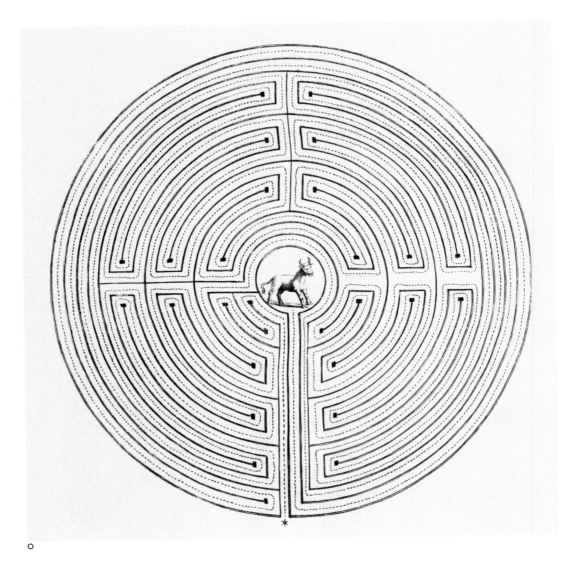

○

The Cosmic Dance

'I thought of a labyrinth of labyrinths, of one sinuous spreading labyrinth that would encompass the past and the future and in some way involve the stars.'

Jorge Luis Borges, 'The Garden of the Forking Paths', 1941

The Cosmic Dance

○
Intricate radial tile patterning decorating the
interior of a dome of the Shah Jahan mosque,
Thatta, Sindh, Pakistan, 1647

□
Illustration from a collection of geometric
and perspective drawings in the Herzog
August Bibliothek, 16th century

□

'I love the simplicity of the cube because it's a very clear geometrical shape, and I love geometry because it's the study of how the whole universe is structured.'

Erno Rubik, quoted in CNN article 'The little cube that changed the world', 2012

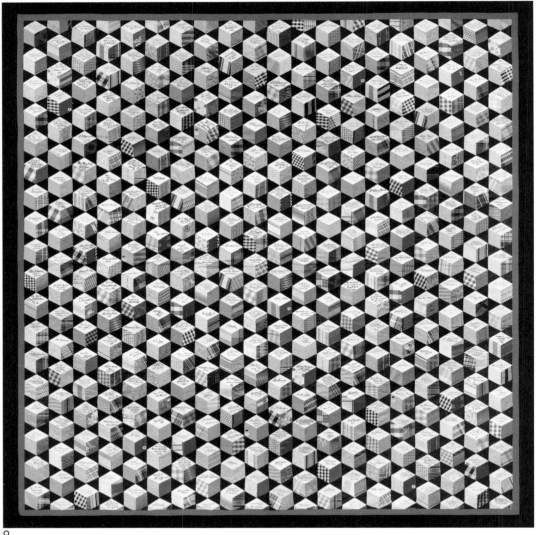

The Cosmic Dance

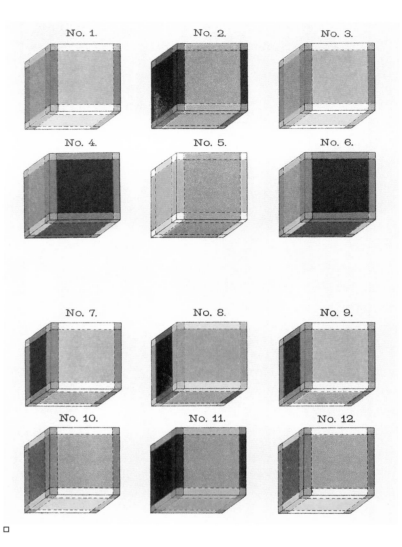

No. 1.   No. 2.   No. 3.
No. 4.   No. 5.   No. 6.
No. 7.   No. 8.   No. 9.
No. 10.   No. 11.   No. 12.

○
Quilt, tumbling blocks with signatures
pattern, including autographs of eight
US presidents and key figures from
the scientific and artistic worlds,
Adeline Harris Sears, begun in 1856

□
Frontispiece depicting coloured cubes,
or tesseracts, from *The Fourth Dimension*,
Charles Howard Hinton, 1904

○

'I chance to think that all nature
and the graceful sky are symbolized
in the art of Geometria.'

Johannes Kepler, *Tertius interveniens*, 1610

○
Illustration from *Geometria et perspectiva:*
Corpora regulata et irregulata,
Lorenz Stöer, late 16th century

□
Somnium (Ref 5), Laurent Millet, 2015

○

'Clash of a circle with an acute angle of a triangle gives no lesser effect than the approach of the finger of God to the finger of Adam.'

Wassily Kandinsky, quoted in 'Poetry and Painting', 1959

'The world's incessant plan,
Halteth never in one shape,
But forever doth escape,
Like wave or flame, into new forms...'

Ralph Waldo Emerson, *Woodnotes*, 1841

The Cosmic Dance

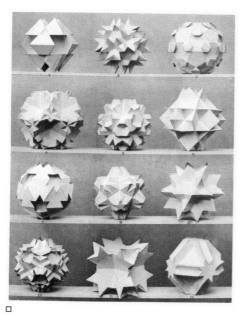

○
Illustration from a collection of geometric and perspective drawings in the Herzog August Bibliothek, 16th century

□
Polyhedra from *Vielecke und Vielflache: Theorie und Geschichte* (*Polygons and Polyhedra: Theory and History*), Max Brückner, 1900

○

A MÖBIUS STRIP is a surface with only one side when embedded in three-dimensional space. It can be constructed by taking a rectangular strip of paper, half-twisting one end of the strip and then reattaching the two ends. By tracing along the surface of the loop with your finger, you will arrive back at your starting point, having traced the entirety of the surface of both sides of the original rectangular strip. Mathematicians August Ferdinand Möbius and Johann Benedict Listing discovered this one-sided surface independently in 1858.

The Cosmic Dance

Möbius Strip I, M. C. Escher, 1961

Sample designs, nos 9, 10, 14 and 38,
from *Prismes: Planches de dessins et coloris,*
E. A. Séguy, 1931

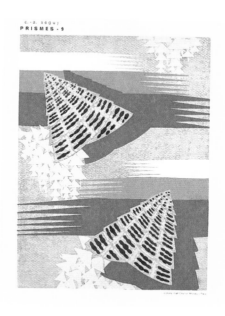

□

'I am not a thing – a noun. I seem
to be a verb, an evolutionary process –
an integral function of the universe.'

Richard Buckminster Fuller, *I Seem To Be A Verb*, 1970

The Cosmic Dance

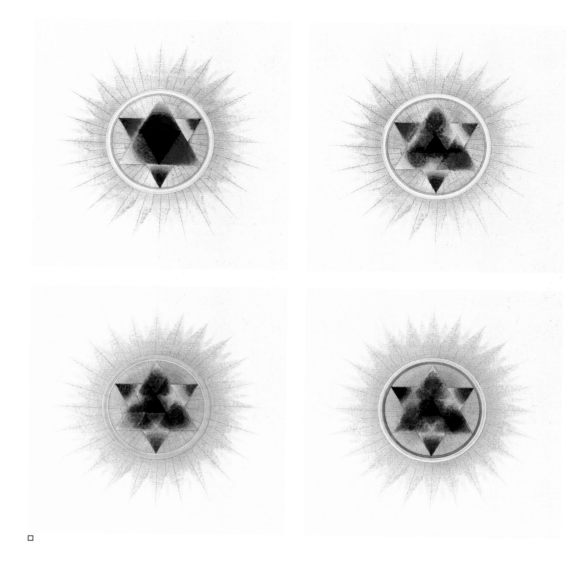

○
Dymaxion House project (plan), Richard Buckminster
Fuller, *c*. 1927

□
Clockwise from top left: 'Diagram of the correlation
of primary colours', 'Diagram of primary colour
harmonies', 'Diagram of tertiary colour harmonies',
'Diagram of secondary colour harmonies', from
*Chromatics, or An Essay on the Analogy and
Harmony of Colours*, George Field, 1817

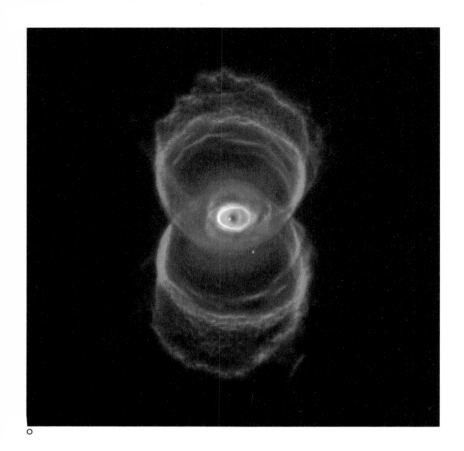

o

'If, like me, you have looked at the stars,
and tried to make sense of what you see,
you too have started to wonder what
makes the universe exist.'

Stephen Hawking, *Stephen Hawking's Universe*, 1997

The Cosmic Dance

○
Hourglass nebula, Hubble telescope photograph
of MyCn18, a young planetary nebula,
16 January 1996

□
Untitled, No. 172, crayon and oil crayon on paper,
Emma Kunz

Divine Proportions

○ □
Design for a cenotaph
for Sir Isaac Newton,
Étienne-Louis Boullée,
1784

○

The Cosmic Dance

NEOCLASSICAL ARCHITECT ÉTIENNE-LOUIS BOULLÉE held that the most beautiful and perfect natural body is the sphere. With his design for a cenotaph for scientist Isaac Newton 50 years after his death, he proposed a massive spherical building 150 m (500 ft) tall, encompassed by two large barriers, encircled by cypress trees. A small sarcophagus is depicted at the base of the sphere. The design is intended to create the effect of day and night. When sunlight penetrates holes in the vaulting, it gives the illusion of stars in the night sky. The day effect is made by an armillary sphere hanging in the centre that emanates a mysterious glow.

'Architecture in itself conveys this idea of limiting space. It's a limit between the finite and the infinite. From this point of view, all architecture is sacred.'

Mario Botta, *American Institute of Architects*, 2008

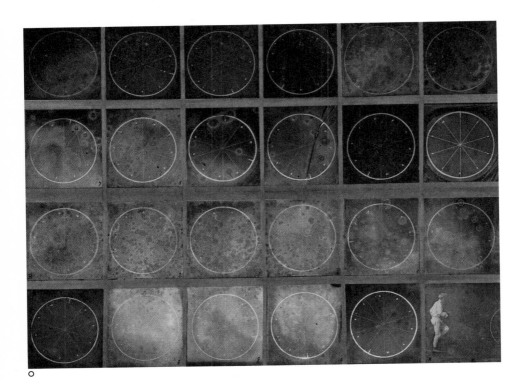

The Cosmic Dance

○
Sequenced image of a rotating sulky
(carriage) wheel and self portrait,
Eadweard Muybridge, c. 1887

□
Colonnade in the Ramalingeshvara Temple,
Rameswaram, Tamil Nadu, photographed
by Nicholas and Company, c. 1884

○

'*Since earth is earth, perhaps, not heaven (as yet)—
Though some savants make earth include the sky;
And blue so far above us comes so high,
It only gives our wish for blue a whet.*'

Robert Frost, 'Fragmentary Blue', 1920

The Cosmic Dance

○

Interior of the Pantheon, Rome (detail),
Giovanni Paolo Pannini, 1706–65

□

Alexander Graham Bell (right) and
his assistants observing the progress
of one of his tetrahedral kites, 1908

Divine Proportions

147

Clockwise from top left: 'The First Knot', 'The Second Knot', 'The Fifth Knot', 'The Fourth Knot', embroidery patterns made of knot work by Albrecht Dürer, after da Vinci, *c.* 1521

The golden dome of the Salon de los Embajadores (Hall of Ambassadors), Alcázar of Seville, Spain

'What power, what force, what mighty spell, if not
Your learned hands, can loose this Gordian knot?'

John Milton, 'At a Vacation Exercise in the College', 1628

CROP CIRCLES are patterns created by flattened areas of crops. It is claimed by some that the first depiction of a crop circle can be found in a 1678 news pamphlet entitled *The Mowing-Devil: or, Strange News Out of Hartfordshire*. Since then, many theories – from air flow patterns and lightning to alien spacecraft – have been proposed to explain the strange phenomenon. The incidence of crop circles increased dramatically in the late 1970s, often close to heritage sites, such as Stonehenge or Avebury. In 1991 hoaxers Doug Bower and Dave Chorley claimed to have started the modern trend in 1978, and demonstrated their art before journalists, using a plank of wood and some rope.

The Cosmic Dance

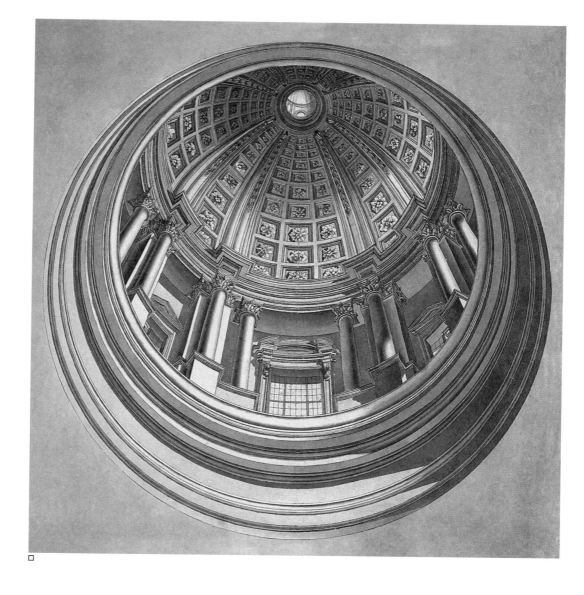

Crop circle, Silbury Hill, Wiltshire, 2009

□
*Perspective Design for a Painted Dome
and Cupola of a Church,* after Andrea
Pozzo, 1700–25

'One is somehow suspended. One is on neutral ground – not in one's own world nor in a strange one. … How stairs do fascinate me when I think of it. Waiting for people – sitting on strange stairs – hearing steps far above… watching someone come up. People come out of themselves on stairs – they issue forth, unprotected.'

Katherine Mansfield, letter to Dorothy Brett, July 1921,
from *Katherine Mansfield Letters and Journals: A Selection*

The Cosmic Dance

○
Illustration from *Perspective,*
Hans Vredeman de Vries, 1604–5

□
'The Drawbridge', plate VII from the
series *Carceri d'invenzione* (*Imaginary
Prisons*), Giovanni Battista Piranesi, 1745

□

'Music of the spheres that builds harmony into atoms, molecules, crystals, shells, suns and galaxies and makes the universe sing.'

Guy Murchie, *The Seven Mysteries of Life*, 1978

The Cosmic Dance

○
Laboratory of the Future,
Man Ray, 1935

□
Kugelobjekt II (Spherical Object II),
Gerhard Richter, 1970

Divine Proportions

○

© Aveez Rahman 2014

MANDELBROT SETS are produced by iteration. In nature, shapes are often composed of iterating patterns – the same pattern repeated on a smaller and smaller scale. For example, a fern is composed of leaves that are each exactly the same shape as the whole plant. Geometric shapes that possess this quality of 'self-similarity' are known as fractals, a word coined in 1975 by mathematician Benoit Mandelbrot (1924–2010). A Mandelbrot set is produced using quadratic polynomials. In 1979 Mandelbrot plotted images of the set on a computer, achieving visualizations of ever more zoomed-in sections of the boundary of the set, revealing self-similar patterns at each step.

'Spider Woman was observant; she watched everything in her environment, and her curiosity focused on a spider weaving a web. This became her plan for how she would weave the universe.'

Barbara Teller Ornelas and Lynda Teller Pete, *Spider Woman's Children: Navajo Weavers Today*, 2018

○
Wearing blanket, Navajo, 1865–75

□
Study for *Camino Real,* Anni Albers, 1967

○

○ Albumen print of Māori wooden club
(*mere*), New Zealand, 1800–99

□ *Marunpa, South of Lake Mackay,*
Pauline Sunfly, 2021

'We remember it all; in our minds, our bodies and feet as we dance the stories. We continually recreate the Tjukurpa.'

Nganyinytja Ilyatjari, 1988

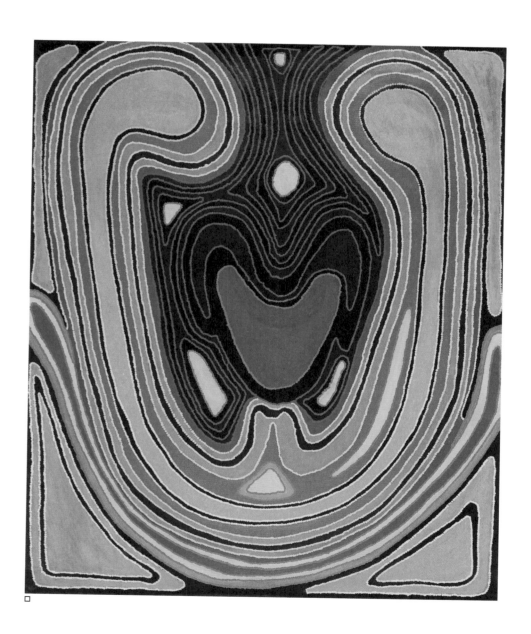

○

A QUINCUNX is a geometrical pattern composed of five points arranged in an X shape so that four of the points form a square or rectangle, with the fifth point at their entre. In the Roman Republic, a quincunx was a coin worth five twelfths of a libra. Kepler lent an astrological meaning to the world when he used it to denote planets that are at an angular distance of five twelfths of a circle (150°) apart. In *The Garden of Cyrus* (1658) physician Sir Thomas Browne outlined the interwoven symbolic meanings of the number 5, the quincunx and the lattice design in nature and art, maintaining that together they were evidence of God's design.

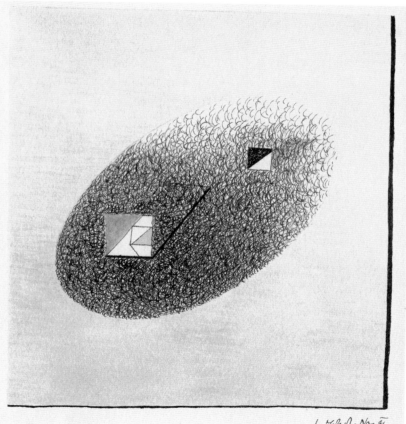

4.
In Search of Nirvana

'And when your soul, the flame, the spark, meets with the divine fuel that is so pure and so strong, it results in immense enlightenment: the enlightenment of God. Light upon light, Noorun Alaa Noor.' ᐃ

○
The Titan's Goblet,
Thomas Cole, 1833

ᐃ
A Blessed Olive Tree: A Spiritual Journey in Twenty Short Stories, Zain Hashmi, 2017

Accoording to the Greek neoplatonist Porphyry (*c.* 234– *c.* 305 CE), the last words of Plotinus to his students were: 'Strive to bring back the god in yourselves to the God in the All.' Plotinus (204/205–270 CE) taught that there was a metaphysical hierarchy of three non-material realities: the One or the Good; *nous* or the Spirit or Intellect; and the Soul or Psyche. The Soul created a physical universe, replicating the beauty and order of the metaphysical reality. It then descended to inhabit individual bodies in the physical world. On the death of the physical body, each individual soul would enter the body of another human or animal. If it had acted badly in one life, it would have to enter a body lower down the hierarchy of beasts. By contrast, if it had acted well, frequently contemplating the beauty of the intellectual realm, achieving moments of ecstasy or union with the One, it could enter a body higher up the hierarchy until eventually it would be able to forget the physical world and become one with *nous* from which it originally derived.

The philosophy of Plotinus was a major influence on Christian and Islamic philosophy. The Holy Trinity of Christian thought – Father, Son and Holy Spirit – is analogous to Plotinus' One, Spirit and Soul. The eternal world of ideas of Plato (*c.* 428/427–348/347 BCE) and Plotinus mirrors the Christians' Kingdom of Heaven – an Other World not metaphysically different from the world of matter but existing in the future. Multiple heavens are described in Jewish apocryphal literature with paradise – the state in which the righteous enjoy spiritual fulfilment – numbering either the third of seven heavens or the seventh of ten. According to Jewish belief, every individual is resurrected after death and subjected to a final judgment with the righteous destined for paradise and the unrighteous to a place of punishment, called Gehenna. Early Vedic texts also speak of an afterlife in heaven or hell, depending on the cumulative virtues or vices performed in life. Vedic philosophers also believed that when the sum of merit had been exhausted the individual soul is reborn.

In the Catholic Church during the Middle Ages the concept of purgatory became established: a place where the dead might go immediately after death to atone for their lesser sins or be punished for their mortal sins before proceeding to heaven and becoming reconciled with God. Based on the teachings

o

of St Thomas Aquinas (1225–1274), the poem
Divina Commedia by Dante Alighieri (1265–
1321) traces the journey of the individual soul,
in the form of the pilgrim Dante, through the
nine circles each of Hell, Purgatory and Heaven.
A similar concept, known as *karma,* is found
in classical Buddhism. It taught that the soul
could be reborn in any of the six realms – as
a god, human, demigod, animal, hungry ghost
or hell being – depending on the actions of
the individual in their previous life.

   The achievement of mystical union with
God was central to Kabbalah, which emerged
in the Jewish tradition in the 13th century.
Kabbalists believe that every human being is a
divine microcosm and the spiritual realms are
the divine macrocosm. During the Renaissance,
Christians and Hermeticists developed their
own forms of Kabbalah. Hermeticists based
their beliefs on the writings (*c.* 100–*c.* 300 CE)
attributed to Hermes Trismegistus, translated
by Marsilio Ficino (1433–1499) and Lodovico
Lazzarelli (1447–1500), and on Paracelsus'
(1494–1541) medical texts. These drew on
astrology, alchemy and magic – 'the three parts
of the wisdom of the whole universe', referred
to in the hermetic text, the *Emerald Tablet.* In
the 17th century, the Rosicrucians incorporated
Hermetic philosophy, Kabbalah and divine
magic in their secret practices. The Order is
symbolized by the rose, which represents the
soul, and the cross, representing the body.
Practitioners seek to attain greater knowledge
and spiritual enlightenment while remaining
in the physical body.

   In Hinduism, Buddhism, Jainism and
Sikhism the ultimate aim is nirvana – liberation
from worldly suffering and the end of the
repeating cycle of rebirth. According to Hindu

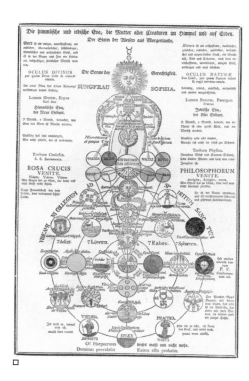

philosophy, nirvana is the union of Atman,
or self, with Brahman, or the cosmic principle.
In Buddhism the Four Noble Truths and the
Eightfold Path teach believers how to reach a
state of non-self and emptiness. For Buddhists
freedom from suffering entails overcoming
all forms of desire, which can be achieved by
practising concentration meditation; liberation
from rebirth can be attained by practising
insight meditation. Mandalas are used as an
aid to these meditations. A monk might achieve
nirvana during his life on Earth – complete
freedom from desire and peace of mind.
Nirvana achieved after death is the complete
absence of consciousness.

'So on he fares, and to the border comes
Of Eden, where delicious Paradise,
Now nearer, crowns with her enclosure green,
As with a rural mound the champaign head
Of a steep wilderness…'

John Milton, *Paradise Lost*, BOOK IV, 1667

The Cosmic Dance

○
Detail of a miniature of a garden or flowery
field, Pacino di Buonaguida, from *Address
to Robert of Anjou, King of Naples from
the Town of Prato in Tuscany*, c. 1335–40

□

Paradise, Herri met de Bles, c. 1541–50

In Search of Nirvana

LOTUS FLOWERS drop seeds that can lay dormant in the dried basins of ponds and rivers for years – 1300 years in one recorded case – before germinating. Rooted in deep mud, the flower of the lotus blooms above water, submerging below water every evening and rising and blooming again the next morning. Consequently, in many Eastern cultures it is a symbol of miraculous life and rebirth, and of the potential to overcome obstacles of the material world and become enlightened. The Buddha is sometimes depicted sitting on a lotus flower and the Hindu goddess Lakshmi, who is associated with fertility, is almost always pictured sitting on one. In Hindu iconography, the flower is often used to express spiritual promise, with its unfolding petals suggesting the expansion of the soul.

The Cosmic Dance

Mural depicting the doctrine of
the Buddha blossoming like a lotus,
Wat Bowonniwet Vihara, Bangkok,
Thailand, by Khrua In Khong, 1865

□
The Garden of Earthly Delights
(detail from centre panel),
Hieronymus Bosch, *c.* 1490–1510

In Search of Nirvana

○
Assumption of the Virgin,
Parma Cathedral, Correggio,
1526–30

□
Mundus subterraneous (above)
and *Pyrophylaciorum* (below),
Athanasius Kircher, 1665

The Cosmic Dance

'Lord, when thou didst ascend on high,
Ten thousand angels filled the sky.'

Isaac Watts, from a hymn relating to Psalm 68, the Bible

○

○
*The Archangel Michael Weighing
the Souls of the Dead*, Juan de la
Abadía the Elder, *c.* 1480–95

□
*Yaksa Form of Vajrapani
(Blue Fudo)*, Japan, Kamakura
period, 13th–14th century

The Cosmic Dance

'*Depart from me, you cursed, into the eternal fire prepared for the devil and his angels.*'

The Bible, Matthew 25:41

○

'A dungeon horrible, on all sides round
As one great furnace flamed, yet from those flames
No light, but rather darkness visible
Served only to discover sights of woe,
Regions of sorrow, doleful shades, where peace
And rest can never dwell, hope never comes.'

John Milton, *Paradise Lost*, BOOK I, 1667

The Cosmic Dance

○
Christ's Descent into Hell,
follower of Hieronymus Bosch,
c. 1525–50

In Search of Nirvana

○

○
Pavement design with Medusa head,
Sousse Region, Tunisia,
2nd–3rd century CE

□
Photograph of grotesque figure,
Parco dei Mostri (Park of the Monsters),
Bomarzo, Lazio, Italy, Herbert List, 1952

The Cosmic Dance

'Crowning the shield was the grim mask of Gorgo, glaring fearfully, with Terror and Panic on either side… along it there wound an enamel snake.'

Homer, *The Iliad, c.* 8th century BCE

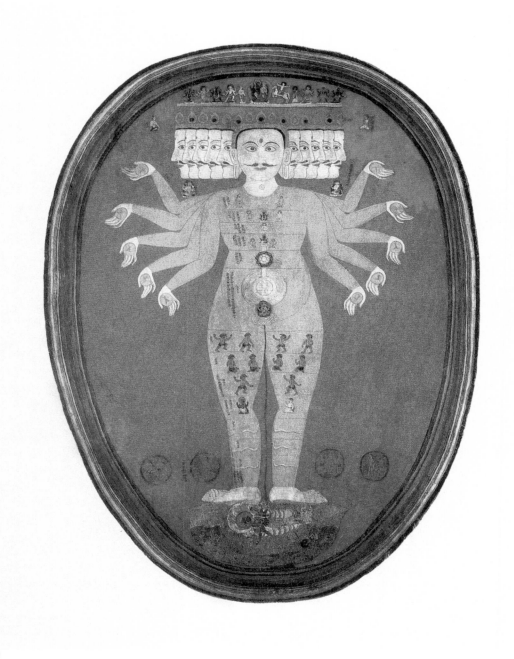

o

The Cosmic Dance

○
Watercolour of Purusha, the thousand-
headed Cosmic Man, standing on Vishnu,
Nepal, 17th century

□
Watercolour of a thousand-headed
Vishnu from a *Bhagavata Purana*
manuscript, Jaipur, Rajasthan, *c.* 1830

VISHNU IS ONE OF THE TRINITY OF DEITIES of Hinduism that
together represent different aspects of the supreme being and
individually represent the key forces of the cyclic succession of the
universe. Brahma is the creator of the universe, Vishnu the preserver
and Shiva the destroyer. Vishnu is usually depicted with dark blue
skin and four arms, carrying a conch, *chakra*, lotus flower and mace.
In his supreme form Vishnu becomes Vishvarupa, or Cosmic Man,
who contains the infinite universe with all its creatures within him
and has innumerable forms, eyes, faces, mouths and arms.

A MANDALA, MEANING 'CIRCLE' IN SANSKRIT, is a geometric design, incorporating key symbols and often surrounded by important figures, used in many Eastern religions, including Buddhism and Hinduism, as an aid to meditation and spiritual discovery. A mandala can represent the universe in miniature, the Pure Land of enlightenment or a specific deity. In Hinduism a simple mandala is known as a yantra. Contemplation of its complex patterns, starting from the outside and moving inwards, and following its associated texts, or tantras, facilitates a transformative journey for the reader.

　　　　The Cosmic Dance

○

Thangka depicting thirteen mandalas
from the Vairocana Cycle,
15th century

□

Yantra of the goddess Pratyangira,
Gujarat, India, *c.* 1700–50

In Search of Nirvana

Merging of Shiva and Shakti, Rajasthan, India, 20th century

Illuminated page from *Biblia pauperum* (*Paupers' Bible*), 1414–15

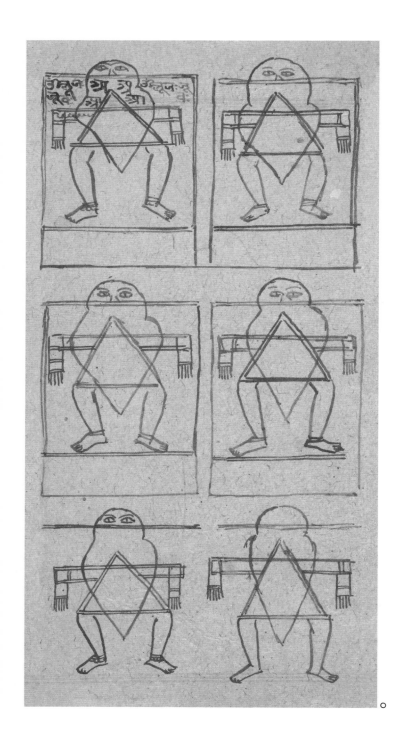

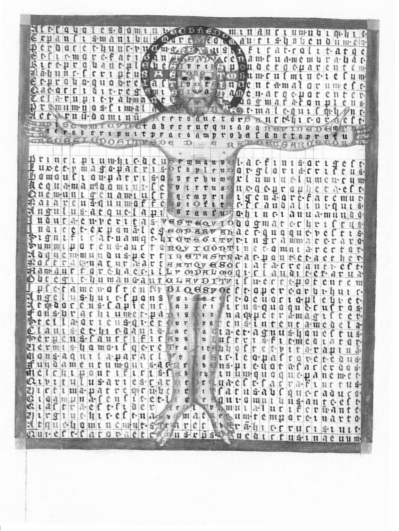

> 'God Shiva and his mountain bride,
> Like word and meaning unified,
> The world's great parents.'

Kalidasa, *Raghuvamsa*, c. 5th century, translated by Arthur W. Ryder

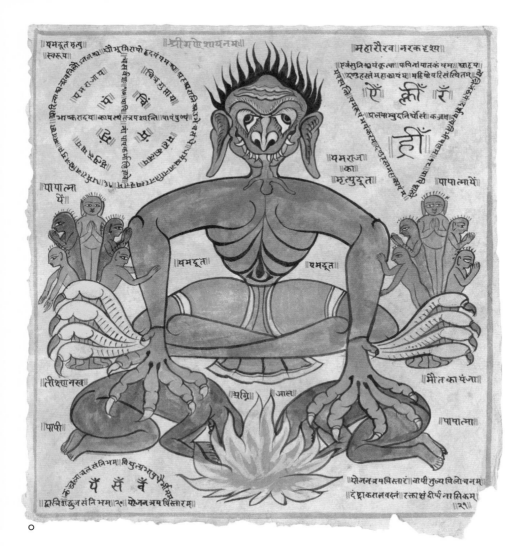

o

'Everything goes, everything comes back;
the wheel of being rolls eternally.
Everything dies, everything blossoms again.'

Friedrich Nietzsche, *Thus Spoke Zarathustra*, 1883, translated by Adrian Del Caro

The Cosmic Dance

□

'These hells, and hundreds and thousands of others,
are the places in which sinners pay the penalty
of their crimes. As numerous as are the offences
that men commit, so many are the hells in
which they are punished.'

'Divisions of Naraka', *The Vishnu Purana,* translated by Horace Hayman Wilson, 1840

The Cosmic Dance

Diagrams of the Universe: The Two-and-a-Half Continents, Gujarat, 1613

Jain cosmological diagram of the world of mortals, *c.* 1850

In Search of Nirvana

o

DESCRIPTIONS OF MYTHICAL BEASTS occur in mythology and folklore all around the world. Some, such as the dragon or tengu, were said to possess magical or supernatural powers, many were used in morality tales to frighten people into behaving virtuously, and some came into being as a result of fanciful descriptions of hitherto unknown real creatures by early travellers. Many are *chimeras*, composed of parts of two or more creatures, such as the griffin – part lion, part eagle – or the faun – part goat, part human. Varieties of many mythical beasts can be found in the mythology of multiple cultures. For example, the Chinese qilin and Japanese kirin bear striking similarity to the European unicorn, and dragon-like beasts can be found in Egyptian, Chinese, Mesopotamian, Indian, ancient Greek and Roman cultures. In medieval times, illustrated bestiaries, describing a great number of beasts – both real and fictional – became popular in Europe. They described the symbolic meaning of each creature and often also provided an accompanying moral lesson.

The Cosmic Dance

Illustration of alchemical beast from
Clavis artis, attributed to Zoroaster,
late 17th or early 18th century

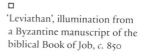
'Leviathan', illumination from
a Byzantine manuscript of the
biblical Book of Job, *c.* 850

'This animal is as large as a full-grown horse. …
It is exceedingly swift of foot. Between its brows
there ſtands a single black horn, not smooth
but with certain natural rings, and tapering
to a very sharp point.'

Aelian, *On the Nature of Animals*, c. 2nd–3rd century, quoted in *The Lore of the Unicorn*, 1930

○
Golden bird from *The Ripley Scroll,*
c. 16th century

□
The Unicorn in Captivity (tapestry),
Master of the Hunt of the Unicorn, *c.* 1500

□

The Cosmic Dance

'He is the heart of every creature;
He is the meaning of each feature;
And his mind is the sky.'

Ralph Waldo Emerson, *Woodnotes*, 1841

o

'He has a frightful face, the neck great and
hairy, he has the breast before square, hardy
and pugnacious; his shape behind is slender,
his tail of large fashion, he has the feet large
and cloven, the claws long and curved.'

Philippe de Thaon, *The Beastiary* (description of a lion), *c.* 1121, translated by Thomas Wright

The Cosmic Dance

□

○
'The Cosmic Rose', scheme of Christian Kabbalism, from *Amphitheatrum sapientiae aeternae* (*Amphitheatre of Eternal Wisdom*), 1595

□
Illustration of the Universal Spirit of Nature from *A Key to Physic, and the Occult Sciences*, Ebenezer Sibly, 1794

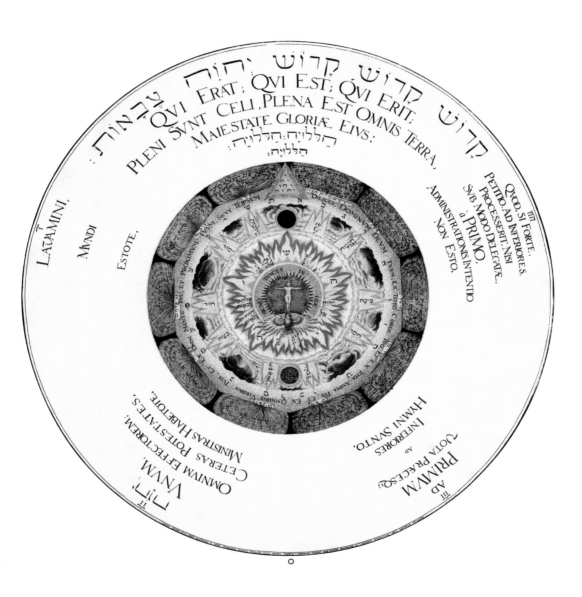

The Cosmic Dance

□

ROSICRUCIANISM is a spiritual movement that announced itself
in Europe with the publication of three anonymous manifestos
between 1614 and 1617. They described a previously unknown
esoteric order supposedly founded around 1407 by a German
physician and mystic called Christian Rosenkreuz. It took as its
symbol an image of a red cross surmounted by a rose – the rosy
cross. The purpose of the order was 'universal reformation of
mankind' through use of ancient mystical and alchemical practices.
The order influenced many occult philosophers of the 17th century,
including Robert Fludd, and subsequent secret societies, such
as Freemasonry and the Hermetic Order of the Golden Dawn.

o

THE WHEEL OF FORTUNE belongs to the Roman goddess Fortuna,
goddess of luck and fate. She is generally depicted with a wheel or
ball, a cornucopia and a ship's rudder. She can bring good or bad luck
with the random turn of her wheel and is often shown blindfolded.
The metaphor of the wheel of fortune was popularized in the Middle
Ages through wide reading of *The Consolation of Philosophy* (52 CE)
by Boethius, which was translated into Italian by Alberto della Piagentina
in 1332 and into English by Chaucer in 1478. Boethius' philosophical
discussion regarding the fickle nature of fate and the relationship
of chance to free will chimed with Christians during this period, who
comprehended the occurrence of apparently random events as part
of God's hidden plan, which humankind should not try to change.

○
The Spiritual Crown of Annie Mary
Howitt Watts, Georgiana Houghton, 1867

□
The Beginning of Life (Water Lilies),
Frantisek Kupka, *c.* 1900

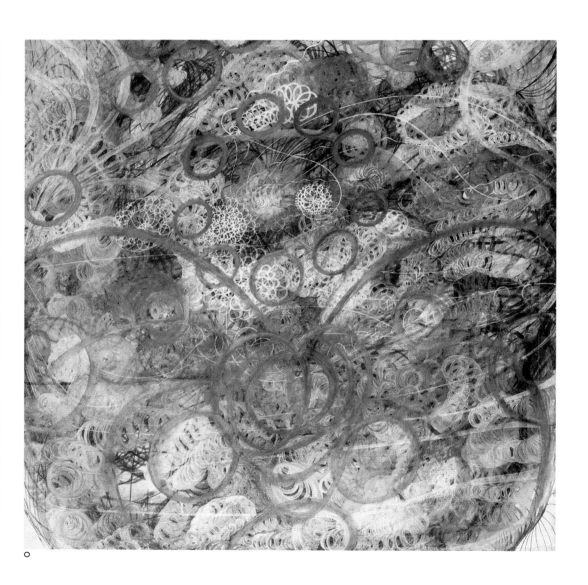

○

The Cosmic Dance

'Angels, living light most glorious! Beneath the Godhead in burning desire in the darkness and mystery of creation you look on the eye of your God never taking your fill: What glorious pleasures take shape within you!'

Hildegard von Bingen, *Symphonia*, c. 1151–58, translated by Mark Atherton

○
Grindelwald. Grotte de Glace, Charnaux
Frères & Cie, *c.* 1880–90

□
Grotto of Sarrazine near Nans-sous-
Sainte-Anne, Gustave Courbet, *c.* 1864

The Cosmic Dance

'Consider… one was freed from his fetters and compelled to stand up suddenly and turn his head around and walk and to lift up his eyes to the light, and… because of the dazzle and glitter of the light, was unable to discern the objects whose shadows he formerly saw.'

Plato, 'Parable of the Cave', *The Republic*, c. 375 BCE, translated by Paul Shorey

o

The Cosmic Dance

○
Adiantum pedatum (Maidenhair Fern,
Young Unfurling Fronds Enlarged 8 Times),
Karl Blossfeldt, gelatin silver print, 1924–32

□
Illustration of an Aztec solar calendar from *Descripción*
histórica y cronológica de las dos piedras que hallaron
en ella el año de 1790 (A Historical and Chronological
Description of Two Stones, Which Were Found in the
Principle Square of Mexico, During the Current Paving
Project), Antonio de León y Gama, printed 1792

COELI
CHRISTI
SPHÆRIUM

5.

And So On To Infinity

'A few quadrillions of eras,
a few octillions of cubic
leagues, do not hazard the
span or make it impatient,
They are but parts,
any thing is but a part.
See ever so far, there is
limitless space outside of that,
Count ever so much, there
is limitless time around that.' [△]

○
Harmonia macrocosmica,
Andreas Cellarius, 1660

△
Walt Whitman, 'Song of Myself'
from *Leaves of Grass,* 1891–92

Early attempts at mapping the structure of the universe were made by the ancient Egyptians 5,000 years ago when the falcon god Horus was said to have conquered the god of chaos, Set, and the concept of divine kingship was established. Observing the movement of the sun across the horizon, Egyptians surmised that the sky goddess, Nut, gave birth to the sun god, Ra, once a year. They developed a calendar by dividing the 360° ecliptic into 36 sections – each identified by a group of stars – of 10° each, known as decans. The rising of consecutive decans on the horizon marked decan hours and groups of 10 days, resulting in 360 days in a year. The Egyptians added five extra days to this to equate to a solar year of 365 days.

In Mesopotamia, from Sumerian times, priests attempted to equate events on Earth with specific positions of the planets and stars. From 1830 BCE onwards Babylonian astronomers recorded observations relating to celestial phenomena. By daily recording the positions of the planets, the rising and setting of the moon, and the appearance of eclipses, they formulated a twelve-month calendar based on the lunar cycles and they calculated how to predict eclipses, which they believed could foretell the death of a king. From c. 1200 BCE, astronomers collated star catalogues, listing constellations, stars and planets in the zodiac – the section of the sky that extends approximately 8° north or south of the ecliptic. The earliest Babylonian star catalogue, known as *Three Stars Each*, divides the heavens into three equal parts: a northern hemisphere belonging to the god of wind, air and earth, Enlil; an equator, ruled by Anu, the supreme god; and a southern hemisphere belonging to Enki, the god of water, knowledge and creation. The sun spent three consecutive months in each third. There are 36 stars listed in the catalogue, three for each month.

The most extensive and accurate record of comets were made by the ancient Chinese, from 613 BCE. Comets have always been considered a bad omen, signalling the impending death of a king or another disaster. Aristotle (384–322 BCE) thought that comets were created from a mixture of the four elements and emanated from the upper atmosphere of the Earth. It was not until 1577 CE, when Tycho Brahe (1546–1601) was able to chart the course of a comet precisely in the skies above Europe, that it was proved that comets travelled through space.

Babylonian star catalogues found their way to ancient Greece in the 4th century BCE, but it was not until the establishment of

Nunc quoque cõfuse qm nota pua figura
Ante quod est in me p:uisq; videatur.

○
Illumination, showing the double Janus, looking at the four parts of the world, from *La Cité de Dieu* (VOL. I) by Augustine, translated by Raoul de Presles, *c.* 1475

□
'System According to the Holy Scriptures' from *Two Systems of Astronomy,* drawn by Isaac Frost, printed by G. Baxter, engraved by W. P. Chubb & Son, 1846

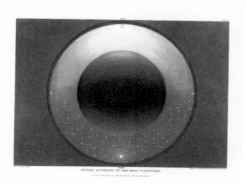

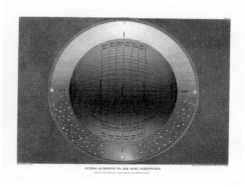

□

Alexandria as the centre of Greek culture in Ptolemaic Egypt after 305 BCE that Babylonian astrology was combined with Egyptian decanic astrology and Greek planetary gods and the four elements to create horoscopic astrology. Alexandrian scholar Claudius Ptolemy (*c.* 100– *c.* 170 CE) set out the rationale and principles of this astrology in a text known as *Tetrabiblos,* which later became the basis of Renaissance astrology. Ptolemy was also responsible for a treatise on astronomy known as the *Almagest.* Using astronomical observations made over 800 years, together with his own observations using an early astrolabe, he constructed a geocentric model of the universe in which the sun, moon, planets and stars all orbit Earth. He held that the Earth was spherical rather than flat and that the movement of the planets was circular. He also included tables by which to calculate the future position of the planets and a star catalogue of 48 constellations.

It was not until the 16th century that astronomer and cleric, Nicolaus Copernicus (1473–1543), established the heliocentric model of the universe. In *On the Revolutions of the*

Heavenly Spheres (1543) he proposed that the Earth is another planet and that all the planets orbit a fixed sun in a circular motion, the Earth revolving once around the sun in the course of a year and turning on its axis once a day. Johannes Kepler (1571–1630) improved on Copernicus' theory by suggesting in *Astronomia nova* (1609) that the movement of the planets was elliptical and not circular and in 1687 Isaac Newton (1642–1727) proposed universal gravity and the law of gravitational attraction, which supported Kepler's theory, completing the Copernican Revolution.

In 1925 it was established beyond doubt that the Milky Way containing our solar system constitutes just one of many galaxies in the universe. Using the world's largest telescope at Mount Wilson Observatory in California, Edwin Hubble (1889–1953) captured photographs of distant spiral nebulae, revealing them to be composed of innumerable individual stars. Today it is known that there are approximately 200 billion galaxies in the observable universe and that the entire universe is constantly expanding.

And So On To Infinity

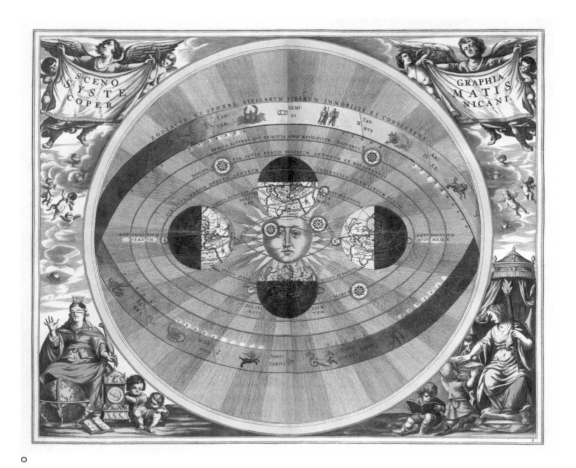

'In the vaſt cosmical changes, the universal
life comes and goes in unknown quantities. …
Enormous gearing, whose firſt motor is the
gnat, and whose laſt wheel is the zodiac.'

Victor Hugo, *Les Misérables*, 1862, translated by Charles E. Wilbour

The Cosmic Dance

‘Scenographia systematis Copernicani’ from
Harmonia macrocosmica (*Celestial Atlas of
Universal Harmony*), Andreas Cellarius, 1660

Plates of celestial map (above) and
armillary sphere (below), Ahmed al-Kirimi,
from *Jihannuma,* Katip Çelebi, 1732

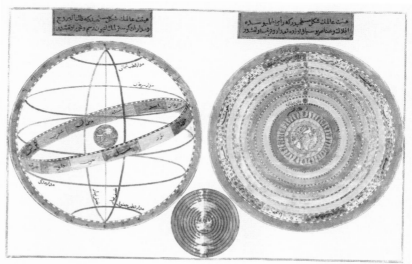

o

THE DIVISION OF THE ZODIAC (the belt of sky visible from Earth as it orbits the sun) into twelve signs can be traced to Babylonian astronomers of the first millennium BCE. The ancient Egyptian Dendera zodiac, dating to 50 BCE, is the first known depiction of the twelve signs, each representing 30° of celestial longitude and corresponding to a star constellation. Some of its icons are familiar Greco-Roman forms, such as the ram and the bull, while others are Egyptian, such as the god Hapy for Aquarius. It was the Alexandrian astrologer Ptolemy who, in the second century CE, codified the system with ruling planets and houses.

The Cosmic Dance

○
Surya Surrounded by the Signs of the Zodiac,
Himachal Pradesh Pahari School, India, *c.* 1830

◻
Illustration of the Dendera zodiac (a bas-relief
on the ceiling of the Hathor temple at Dendera
in Egypt), 19th century

◻

'The soul
of the newly
born baby
is marked
for life by
the pattern
of the stars
at the moment
it comes into
the world,
unconsciously
remembers it,
and remains
sensitive to
the return of
configurations
of a similar
kind.'

Johannes Kepler,
Harmonices mundi, 1619

The Cosmic Dance

○
Detail of illumination
of Pisces from folio
30v of *Metali'ü's-sa'adet
ve-yenabi'ü's-siyadet*,
Seyyid Muhammed bin
Emir Hasan el-Saudî, 1582

□
Detail of illumination
of Leo from folio 16v
of *Metali'ü's-sa'adet ve-
yenabi'ü's-siyadet*, Seyyid
Muhammed bin Emir
Hasan el-Saudî, 1582

And So On To Infinity

'Heaven walks among us ordinarily
muffled in such triple or tenfold
disguises that the wisest are deceived
and no one suspects the days to be gods.'

Ralph Waldo Emerson, letter to Margaret Fuller, 1840

The Cosmic Dance

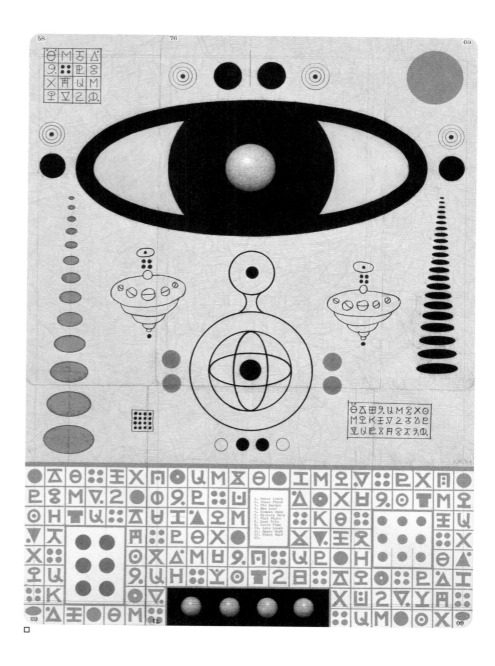

○
Detail of illustration of Kalachakra
cosmology, showing the twelve tracks
on which the sun revolves around
Mount Meru, 16th century

□
Cosmic Map, Bruno Munari, 1930

○

The Cosmic Dance

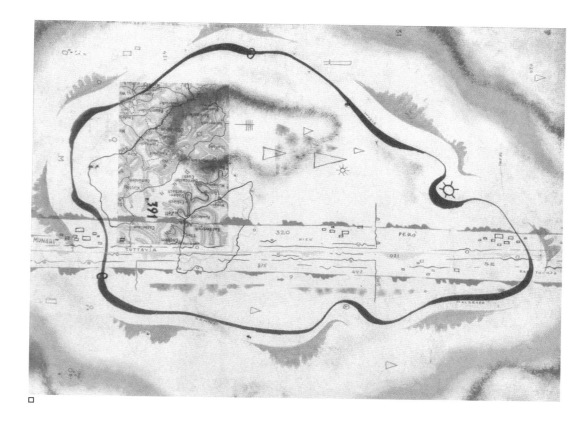

THE FIRST MAPS OF THE UNIVERSE depict a flat Earth lying beneath a hemispherical firmament. In the 6th century BCE, in ancient China, *gai tian* or 'canopy heaven' was proposed in which the heavens were conceived as a flat plane parallel to the Earth. The ancient Greeks determined that the Earth was spherical and favoured a geocentric model of the universe, which was established by Alexandrian astronomer Ptolemy (*c.* 100–*c.* 170 CE) in the *Almagest* (*c.* 150 CE). Early Islamic astronomers portrayed the Earth as being in the centre of eight spheres, in which the outer, revolving, sphere consisted of the stars. Although Aristarchus of Samos proposed a heliocentric system in *c.* 270 BCE in which the Earth and other celestial bodies orbited the sun, it was not until Nicolaus Copernicus' (1473–1543) proposal of a heliocentric cosmos in *On the Revolutions of the Heavenly Spheres* (1543) that this model was seriously examined.

○ Star map, Korea, 14th century

□ Star chart from *Heitengi zuka,*
Yoshitaka Iwahashi, 1802

The Cosmic Dance

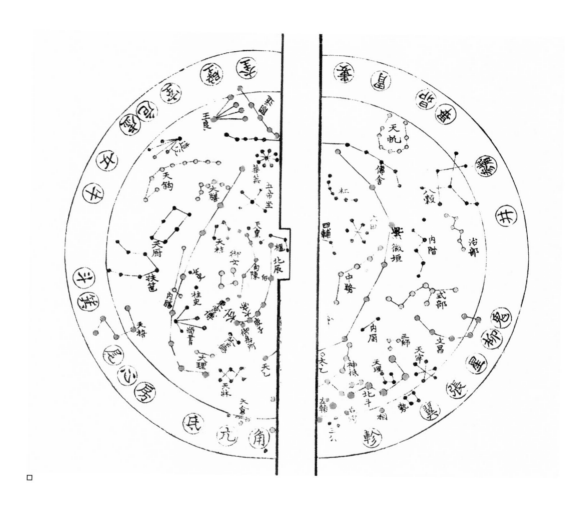

'The stars are like letters that inscribe themselves
at every moment in the sky. ... Everything in the
world is full of signs. ... All events are coordinated.'

Plotinus, *Enneads*, *c.* 268 CE, translated by C. Jackson and J. Allen

'In every Instant being begins;
around every Here rolls the ball
There. The middle is everywhere.
Crooked is the path of eternity.'

Friedrich Nietzsche, *Thus Spoke Zarathustra*, 1883,
translated by Adrian Del Caro

The Cosmic Dance

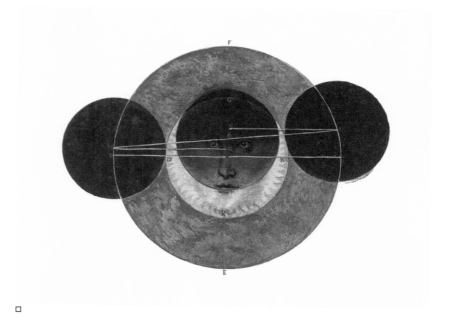

○
Illustration from *Das Wunderzeichenbuch*
(*The Book of Miracles*), 1552

□
Illustrations from *Eclipses luminarium*,
Cyprian Leowitz, 1555

○

Diagrams showing the orbits
of the sun and the moon from
*De Natura avium; de pastoribus
et ovibs; bestiarium; mirabilia
mundi; philosophia mundi:
On the Soul*, Franco-Flemish,
1277 or after

□

Illustration of the sun and
the moon from *Livre de
la Vigne nostre Seigneur*,
France, *c.* 1450–70

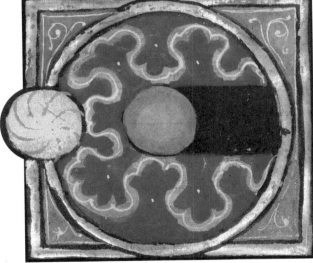

○

'If you could see the earth illuminated
when you were in a place as dark
as night, it would look to you more
splendid than the moon.'

Galileo Galilei, *Dialogue Concerning the Two Chief World Systems*, 1632

And So On To Infinity

LVNA.

O

'And God made two great lights,
great for their use
To man, the greater to have rule by day,
The less by night...'

John Milton, *Paradise Lost*, BOOK VII, 1667

○

'Luna' ('Moon') from *Description of the Eight Pageants Held during the Games on the Occasion of the Christening of Princess Elisabeth of Hesse*, 1596

□

'Sol' ('Sun') from *Description of the Eight Pageants Held during the Games on the Occasion of the Christening of Princess Elisabeth of Hesse*, 1596

□

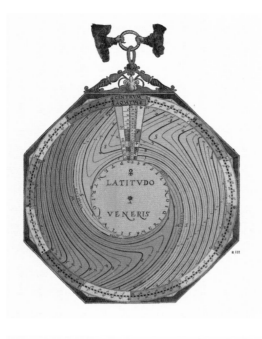

o

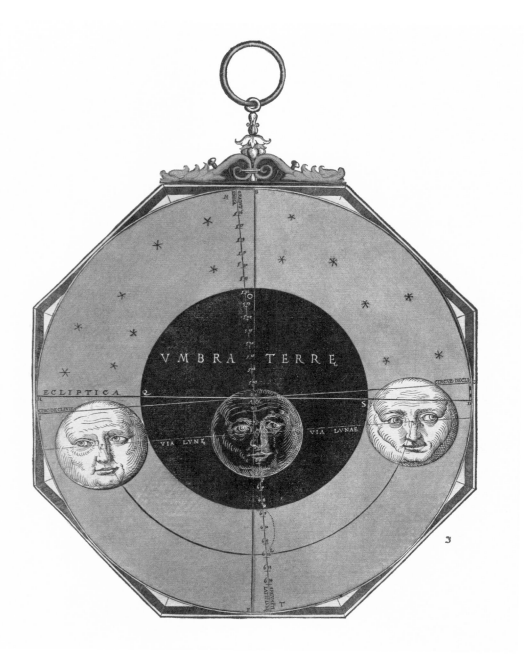

○□
Volvelles, or wheel charts, designed to calculate phases
of the sun and moon, positions of the planets and
eclipses, created by Michael Ostendorfer and reproduced
in *Astronomicum Caesareum* by Petrus Apianus, 1540

And So On To Infinity

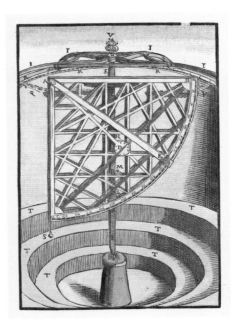

Illustrations from *Astronomiae instauratae mechanica*, Tycho Brahe, 1598

'Astronomy' from *The Cabinet Maker and Artist's Encyclopedia*, Thomas Sheraton, 1805

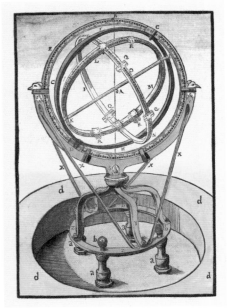

The Cosmic Dance

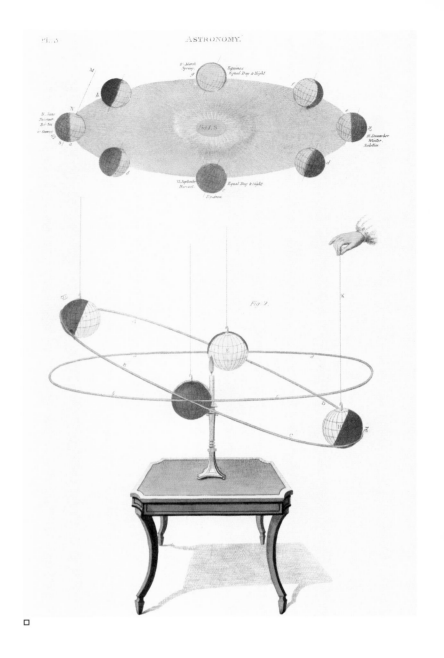

'*For all these years you were merely*
A smear of light through our telescopes.'

Stuart Atkinson, 'Lutetia in the Light', 2010

○

'Deep in the shady sadness of a vale
Far sunken from the healthy breath of morn,
Far from the fiery noon, and eve's one star,
Sat gray-hair'd Saturn, quiet as a stone,
Still as the silence round about his lair.'

John Keats, 'Hyperion', 1818

O

○
Representations of galaxies from
*An Original Theory or New Hypothesis
of the Universe*, Thomas Wright, 1750

□
'The Newtonian System of the Universe',
drawn by Isaac Frost, engraved by W. P.
Chubb & Son, printed by G. Baxter, 1855

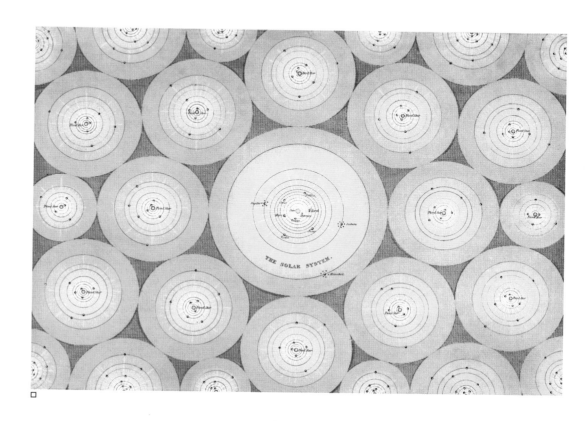

*'There is a single general space, a single
vaſt immensity which we may freely
call Void: in it are unnumerable globes
like this on which we live and grow.'*

Giordano Bruno, *On the Infinite Universe and Worlds*, 1584

And So On To Infinity

o

'*Imagine a comet returning centuries hence from the kingdom of the dead, crossing our century tonight and sowing the same seeds...*'

Philippe Jaccottet, *Words in the Air*, 1998, translated by Derek Mahon

The Cosmic Dance

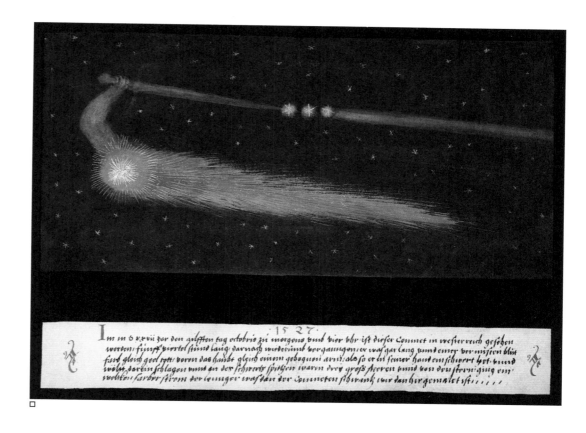

And So On To Infinity

o

'We are no other than a moving row
Of Magic Shadow-shapes that come and go
Round with the Sun-illumined Lantern held
In Midnight by the Master of the Show.'

Omar Khayyam, *The Rubaiyat*, 1120, translated by Edward Fitzgerald

The Cosmic Dance

□

o

'The sun, the sister of the moon, from the south
Her right hand cast over heaven's rim;
No knowledge she had where her home should be,
The moon knew not what might was his,
The stars knew not where their stations were.'

Völuspá, c. 10th century, translated by Henry Adams Bellows

○
Painting of three suns shining simultaneously
in 1533, likely depicting a sun dog illusion,
from *Augsburger Wunderzeichenbuch* (*The
Augsburg Book of Miracles*), 16th century

□
Chart of the signs of the zodiac with Venus,
Cupid and a Bishop Saint, Hans Baldung
Grien, 1484/5–1545

○

○
Night's Plutonian Shore, Gustave Doré
for Edgar Allan Poe's 'The Raven', 1884

□
'The Realm of Chaos and the Night', diagram
of Milton's cosmology from Homer Sprague's
edition of *Paradise Lost*, 1883

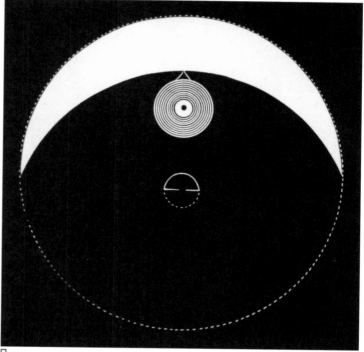

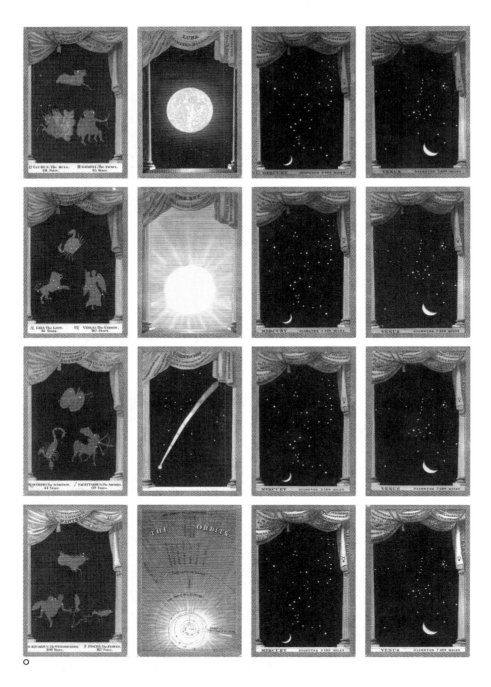

○
Astronomia playing cards, designed
and published by F. G. Moon in London,
England, 1829

□
'Phases of the Moon' from *The Beauty of the
Heavens, A Pictorial Display of the Astronomical
Phenomena of the Universe*, Charles F. Blunt, 1842

'I have seen a thousand moons: harvest moons like gold coins, winter moons as white as ice chips, new moons like baby swans' feathers.'

Gerald Malcolm Durrell, letter to his fiancée Lee, 1978

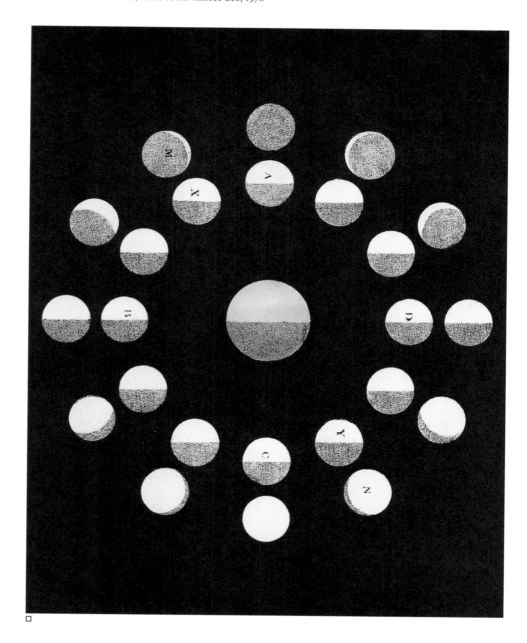

'The Sun is the past, the Earth is the present, the Moon is the future. From an incandescent mass we have originated, and into a frozen mass we shall turn. Merciless is the law of nature, and rapidly and irresistibly we are drawn to our doom.'

Nikola Tesla, 'The Problem of Increasing Human Energy', 1900

The Cosmic Dance

○
Model of the globe exhibited at the Royal
Ontario Museum of Geology and Mineralogy,
Canada, 1950s

□
Model of the moon exhibited at the Field Columbian
Museum, Chicago, Illinois, USA, made by Johann
Friedrich and Julius Schmidt, 1898

Bibliography

Abbott, Berenice, *Documenting Science* (Göttingen: Steidl, 2008)

Albin-Guillot, Laure, *Micrographie Decorative* (Paris: Draeger Freres, 1931)

Aquinas, St. Thomas, *Aurora Consurgens: A Document Attributed to Thomas Aquinas on the Problem of Opposites in Alchemy*, ed. Marie-Louise von Franz, trans. R. F. C. Hull and A. S. B. Glover (New York: Pantheon Books, 1966)
Selected Philosophical Writings, ed. Timothy McDermott (Oxford: Oxford University Press, 2008)

Barkan, Leonard, *Nature's Work of Art: The Human Body as Image of the World* (New Haven: Yale University Press, 1975)

Bashō, Matsuo, *Moon Woke Me Up Nine Times: Selected Haiku of Basho*, trans. David Young (New York: Random House USA, 2013)

Bentley, Wilson A., *Snowflakes in Photographs* (New York: Dover Publications Inc., 2000)

Blair, Sheila and Jonathan Bloom (eds), *God Is Beautiful and Loves Beauty: The Object in Islamic Art and Culture* (New Haven: Yale University Press, 2013)

Blake, William, *William Blake: The Complete Poems*, ed. W. H. Stevenson (London: Longman, 2007)

The Book of Miracles (Das Wunderzeichenbuch) (*c.* 1552), eds Joshua P. Waterman and Till-Holger Borchert (Cologne: Taschen Books, 2017)

Brahe, Tycho, *De mundi aetherei recentioribus phaenomenis liber secundus* (Hven: for the author, 1588)

Brauen, M., *The Mandala: Sacred Circle in Tibetan Buddhism* (London: Serindia Press, 1997)

Broug, Eric, *Islamic Geometric Design* (London: Thames & Hudson, 2013)

Campbell, Joseph, *The Masks of God: Four Volumes* (New York: Viking Press, 1959–68)

Capra, Fritjof, *The Tao of Physics: An Exploration of the Parallels Between Modern Physics and Eastern Mysticism* (Boston: Shambhala, 2010)

Cellarius, Andreas, *Harmonia Macrocosmica* (1660), ed. Robin Van Gent (Cologne: Taschen Books, 2012)

Chladni, Ernst, *Entdeckungen über die Theorie des Klanges* (Leipzig: Weidmanns Erben and Reich, 1787)

Cicero, *De natura deorum* (translation of Aratus of Soli, *Phenomena*), trans. H. Rackham (Edinburgh: William Blackwood & Sons, 1914), II. 110

Cleary, Thomas (ed. and trans.), *I Ching: The Book of Change* (Boston: Shambhala, 2017)

Critchlow, Keith and Seyyed Hossein Nasr, *Islamic Patterns: An Analytical and Cosmological Approach* (London: Thames & Hudson, 2008)

da Vinci, Leonardo, *Notebooks* (Oxford: Oxford University Press, 2008)

Doniger, Wendy (ed. and trans.), *The Rig Veda* (London: Penguin Books, 2005)

Easwaran, E. (ed. and trans.), *The Upanishads* (London: Penguin Books, 1988)

The Egyptian Book of the Dead, ed. John Romer, trans. E. A. Wallis Budge (London: Penguin Books, 2008)

Elfving, Frederik, *Anatomia vegetal* (*Vegetal Anatomy*) (Leipzig: F. E. Wachsmuth, 1929)

Ernst, Bruno, *The Magic Mirror of M. C. Escher* (New York: Random House, 1976)

Erosthathenes and Hyginus, *Constellation Myths with Aratus's* Phaenomena, ed. and trans. Robin Hard (Oxford: Oxford University Press, 2015)

Ettinghausen, Richard, Oleg Grabar and Marilyn Jenkins-Madina, *Islamic Art and Architecture, 650–1250*, 2nd edn (New Haven and London: Yale University Press, 2003)

Fibonacci (Leonardo of Pisa), *Liber abaci* (1202), trans. Laurence Sigler (New York: Springer Verlag, 2003)

Field, George, *Chromatics, or An essay on the analogy and harmony of colours* (London: 1817)

Flammarion, Camille, *Popular Astronomy*, trans. J. Ellard Gore (London: Chatto & Windus, 1894)

Fludd, Robert, *Utriusque cosmi maioris scilicet et minoris metaphysica, physica atque technica historia…* (Frankfurt: for the heirs of J. T. de Bry, by C. Rotelius, 1624)

Fraser, Alec, *A Guide to Operations on the Brain* (London: J. & A. Churchill, 1890)

Fraser, Douglas (ed.), *African Art as Philosophy* (New York: Interbook, 1974)

Frédol, Alfred et al., *Le monde de la mer* (Paris: L. Hachette & Cie, 1866)

Galen, *On the Constitution of the Art of Medicine. The Art of Medicine. A Method of Medicine to Glaucon*, ed. and trans. Ian Johnston (Cambridge, MA: Harvard University Press, 2016)

Galilei, Galileo, *Sidereus nuncius* (*Starry Messenger*) (Venice, IT: Thomas Baglioni, 1610)

Godwin, Joscelyn, *Athanasius Kircher's Theatre of the World* (London: Thames & Hudson, 2009)
Robert Fludd: Hermetic philosopher and surveyor of two worlds (London: Thames & Hudson, 1979)

Graves, Robert, Felix Guirand et al. *The New Larousse Encyclopaedia of Mythology* (London: Hamlyn Books, 1963)

Gray, Henry, *Gray's Anatomy* (Philadelphia, PA: Running Press, 1974)

Grew, Nehemiah, *The Anatomy of Plants. With an Idea of a Philosophical History of Plants. And Several Other Lectures, Read Before the Royal Society* (London: W. Rawlins, 1682)

Haase, Rudolf, Anton Meier et al., *Emma Kunz: Artist, Researcher, Healer* (Würenlos, Switzerland: Emma Kunz Centre, 1998)

Haeckel, Ernst, *Kunstformen der Natur* (*Art Forms of Nature*) (Leipzig and Wien: Bibliographischen Instituts, 1904)

Hesiod, Theogony *and* Works and Days, trans. M. L. West (Oxford: Oxford University Press, 2008)

Hildegard von Bingen, *Selected Writings*, ed. and trans. Mark Atherton (London: Penguin Books, 2005)

Hippocrates, *Hippocratic Writings*, ed. G. Lloyd (London: Penguin Books, 1983)

Hobbes, Thomas, *Leviathan*, ed. Christopher Brooke (London: Penguin Books, 2017)

Hofstadter, Douglas R., *Gödel, Escher, Bach: an Eternal Golden Braid* (New York: Basic Books, 1979)

Hooke, Robert, *Micrographia: or, some physiological descriptions of minute bodies made by magnifying glasses. With observations and inquiries thereupon* (London: The Royal Society, 1665)

Jamme, Franck André (ed.), *Tantra Song: Tantric Painting from Rajasthan* (Los Angeles: Siglio Press, 2011)

Jung, Carl Gustav, M. L. von Franz, Joseph Henderson et al. *Man and His Symbols* (New York: Doubleday & Company Inc., 1969)

The Red Book, ed. Sonu Shamdasani, trans. Mark Kyburz and John Peck (New York: W. W. Norton & Company, 2009)

Kepes, György, *The New Landscape in Art and Science* (Chicago: Paul Theobald & Co., 1956)

Kepler, Johannes, *Harmonice mundi* (*The Harmony of the World*) (Linz: Johann Planck for Gottfried Tampach, 1619)

Kilian, Lucas, *Catoptri microcosmici* (*Mirrors of the Microcosm*), after designs by Dr Johannes Remmelin (Augsburg: Stephan Michelspracher, 1613)

Larsen, Lars Bang et al., *Georgiana Houghton Spirit Drawings* (London: Paul Holberton Publishing, 2016)

Ledermüller, Martin Frobenius, *Amusement microscopique, tant pour l'esprit que pour les yeux* (Nuremberg: Lanoy for Adam Wolfgang Winterschmidt, 1764–68)

Lemagny, Jean-Claude, *Visionary Architects: Boullée, Ledoux, Lequeu* (Los Angeles: Hennessey & Ingalls, 2002)

Leowitz, Cyprian, *Eclipses luminarium* (Augsburg: 1555)

Lucretius, *On the Nature of Things* (*De Rerum Natura*), introd. Richard Jenkyns, trans. A. E. Stallings (London: Penguin Books, 2007)

Lull, Ramón, *Raymundi Lulli Opera Latina* (Strasbourg: Lazarus Zetsner, 1651)

The Mahabharata, ed. John D. Smith (London: Penguin Books, 2009)

Maier, Michael, *Atalanta fugiens* (Oppenheim: Johann Theodori de Bry, 1617)

Malpighi, Marcello, *Anatome plantarum pars altera* (London: Johannis Martyn, 1679)

Mandelbrot, Benoit B., *Fractals: Form, Chance and Dimension* (San Francisco: W. H. Freeman, 1977)

Marks, Robert M., *The Dymaxion World of Buckminster Fuller* (New York: Reinhold Publishing, 1960)

Mazzarello, Paolo, *Golgi: A Biography of the Founder of Modern Neuroscience*, trans. Aldo Badiani and Henry A. Buchtel (Oxford: Oxford University Press, 2010)

Meller, James (ed.), *The Buckminster Fuller Reader* (London: Penguin Books, 1972)

Merian, Maria Sibylla, *Dissertatio de generatione et metamorphosibus insectorum surinamensium* (Amsterdam: J. Oosterwyk, 1719)

Miller, Mary Ellen and Karl Taube, *An Illustrated Dictionary of the Gods and Symbols of Ancient Mexico and the Maya* (London: Thames & Hudson, 1997)

Milton, John, *John Milton: Paradise Lost*, ed. Alastair Fowler (London: Taylor & Francis Ltd, 2006)

Mokerjee, Ajit, *Tantra Art: Its Philosophy and Physics* (New Delhi: Rupa & Co. in collaboration with Ravi Kumar, Paris, 1994)

Muller, Iris, *Hilma af Klint: Painting the Unseen* (Berlin: Hatje Cantz, 2013)

Newton, Isaac, *The Principia: Mathematical Principles of Natural Philosophy*, trans. I. Bernard Cohen and Anne Whitman (Berkeley: University of California Press, 2016)

Ostendorfer, Michael and Petrus Apianus, *Astronomicum Caesareum*, (*The Emperor's Astronomy*) (Ingolstadt: Petrus Apianus, 1540)

Pacioli, Luca and Leonardo da Vinci *De divina proportione* (1509) (Milan: Silvana Editoriale, 1982)

Plato, *The Republic*, ed. and trans. Desmond Lee (London: Penguin Books, 2007)

Pliny the Elder, *Natural History*, trans. John Healey (London: Penguin Books, 1991)

Plotinus, *The Enneads*, ed. John Dillon, trans. Stephen MacKenna (London: Penguin Books, 1991)

The Qur'an, trans. Tarif Khalidi (London: Penguin Books, 2009)

Ramon y Cajal, Santiago, *Textura del sistema nervioso del hombre y de los vertebrados* (Madrid: Nicolás Moya, 1899)

Reuchlin, Johannes, *De arte cabbalistica* (Hagenau: Thomas Anselm, 1517)

Russell, Bertrand, *A History of Western Philosophy and Its Connection with Political and Social Circumstances from the Earliest Times to the Present Day* (London: George Allen and Unwin, 1946)

Schedel, Hartmann, *Liber chronicarum* (*The Nuremberg Chronical*) (Nuremberg: Anton Koberger for Sebald Schreyer and Sebastian Kammermeister, 1493)

Schön, Erhard, *Unterweisung der Proportion und Stellung des Possen* (1542) (Frankfurt: Joseph Baer & Co., 1920)

Sibly, Ebenezer, *A key to physic, and the occult sciences* (1792) (Cambridge: Cambridge University Press, 2012)

Skinner, Stephen et al., *The Splendor Solis: The World's Most Famous Alchemical Manuscript* (London: Watkins Publishing, 2019)

Sowerby, James, *British Mineralogy: or Coloured Figures Intended to Elucidate the Mineralogy of Great Britain* (London: R. Taylor and Co., 1802–17) *Mineral Conchology of Great Britain* (London: Benjamin Meredith, W. Arding, Richard Taylor, 1812–18)

Stöer, Lorenz, *Geometria et perspectiva: Corpora regulata et irregulata* (Augsburg: late 16th century)

Swanson, Larry, Eric Newman, Alfonso Araque and Janet M. Dubinsky, *The Beautiful Brain: The Drawings of Santiago Ramon y Cajal* (New York: Abrams Books, 2017)

The Tibetan Book of Proportions (Palatino Press, 2014)

Tillyard, E. M. W., *The Elizabethan World Picture* (London: Penguin Books, 1972)

Trouvelot, Étienne Léopold, *The Trouvelot Astronomical Drawings Manual* (New York: C. Scribner's Sons, 1881–82)

Tucci, Giuseppe, *The Theory and Practice of the Mandala* (New York: Samuel Weiser Inc., 1973)

Tzu, Lao, *Tao Te Ching*, ed. Paul K. T. Sih, trans. John C. H. Wu (Boston: Shambhala, 1989)

Unterman, Alan, *The Kabbalistic Tradition: An Anthology of Jewish Mysticism* (London: Penguin Books, 2009)

Valmiki, M., *The Ramayana*, trans. Arshia Sattar (London: Penguin Books, 2000)

Vesalius, Andreas, *De humani corporis fabrica libri septem* (Basel: Johannes Oporinus, 1543)

Wright, Thomas, *An Original Theory or New Hypothesis of the Universe…* (London: printed for the author, 1750)

Yates, Frances A., *Giordano Bruno and the Hermetic Tradition* (Chicago: University of Chicago Press, 1964) *The Art of Memory* (London; New York: Routledge and Kegan Paul, 1966) *The Rosicrucian Enlightenment* (London; New York: Routledge and Kegan Paul, 1972)

Zahm, John Augustine, *Sound and Music* (Chicago: A. C. McClurg & Co., 1892)

Sources of Illustrations

Every effort has been made to locate and credit copyright holders of the material reproduced in this book. The author and publisher apologize for any ommissions or errors, which can be corrected in future editions.

Key: a=above, b=below, c=centre, l=left, r=right

1 Pola Von Grüt, *Saturn Return*, 2019. Courtesy the artist; 2 Bayerische Staatsbibliothek Munich, Cod.icon. 181, fol. 69r; 4a *Harmonia macrocosmica sev atlas universalis et novus, totius universi creati cosmographiam generalem, et novam exhibens*, Andreas Cellarius, 1660; 4c *Kristallseelen*, Ernst Haeckel, Leipzig, 1917; 4b akg-images; 5a Heritage Image Partnership Ltd/Alamy Stock Photo; 5ca Rijksmuseum, Amsterdam; 5cb *Harmonia macrocosmica sev atlas universalis et novus, totius universi creati cosmographiam generalem, et novam exhibens*, Andreas Cellarius, 1660; 5b Bibliothèque nationale de France; 7 *Metamorphosis Insectorum Surinamensium*, Maria Sibylla Merian, 1705; 8 British Library Board. All Rights Reserved/Bridgeman Images; 10l The Picture Art Collection/Alamy Stock Photo; 10r *Schedelsche Weltchronik*, Hartmann Schedel, 1493; 11 Old World Auctions; 12 Private Collection; 13 British Library Board. All Rights Reserved/Bridgeman Images; 14 The Art Institute of Chicago/Art Resource, NY/Scala, Florence. © Man Ray 2015 Trust/DACS, London 2022; 15 The J. Paul Getty Museum, Los Angeles, Ms. Ludwig XIII 5, v1, fol. 31; 16 CPA Media Pte Ltd/Alamy Stock Photo; 17 Free Library of Philadelphia/Bridgeman Images; 18 Collection of Alexander Gorlizki; 19 Collection of Alexander Gorlizki; 20 The Bodleian Libraries, University of Oxford, MS. Ashmole 1789, fol. 002v (xii) verso; 21 Bibliothèque nationale de France; 22 *Northern Antiquities*, M. Mallet, Bishop Percy (trans.), 1847; 23 Album/Alamy Stock Photo; 24 Bibliothèque nationale de France; 25 Bibliothèque nationale de France; 26 © Courtesy of the Hilma af Klint Foundation – Photo: Moderna Museet-Stockholm; 27 Heritage Image Partnership Ltd/Alamy Stock Photo; 28 The Picture Art Collection/Alamy Stock Photo; 29 Prahlad Bubbar, London; 30 Heritage Image Partnership Ltd/Alamy Stock Photo; 31 *Le vray et methodiqve covrs de la physiqve resolvtive: vvlgairement dite chymie*, Annibal Barlet, 1657. Yale University Library,

New Haven, Connecticut; 32 Courtesy Gregg Baker Asian Art, Japanesescreens.com; 33 Interfoto/Alamy Stock Photo; 34 Fermilab; 36 *Tout L'univers*, Le Livre de Paris, 1958–1975; 37 Private Collection; 38 *A key to physic, and the occult sciences*, Ebenezer Sibley, 1794. Leeds University Archive; 39 Photo J. P. Wolff; 40 Courtesy of the Department of Special Collections, Stanford University Libraries. Courtesy the estate of György Kepes; 41 Centre Pompidou, Paris, MNAM-CCI, Dist RMN-Grand Palais; 42 *Entdeckungen über die Theorie des Klanges*, Ernst Chladni, 1787; 43 *Sound and Music*, John Augustine Zahm, 1892; 44 © 2022 Adagp Images, Paris/SCALA, Florence. © Succession Yves Klein c/o ADAGP, Paris and DACS, London 2022; 45 *Hamonshū*, Mori Yūzan, 1903; 46 Cosmodernism (Kamil Czapiga), www.instagram.com/cosmodernism; 47 Photo Bernardo Cesare (micROCKScopica); 48 Cosmodernism (Kamil Czapiga), www.instagram.com/cosmodernism; 49 Smithsonian Institution Archives, Washington, DC; 50 Courtesy Kira O'Reilly; 51 Topfoto; 52 Howard Lynk, Victorianmicroscopeslides.com; 53 Eshel Ben-Jacob; 54 California Academy of Sciences, CASG slide no. 351040, CASG slide no. 351069; 55 Scenics & Science/Alamy Stock Photo; 56 Old Books Images/Alamy Stock Photo; 57, 58 Library of Congress, Washington, DC; 59 steeve-x-art/Alamy Stock Photo; 60 peacay; 61 Library of Congress, Washington, DC; 62 Midori Shimoda, Carnival of Onions, 1930s; 63 The Museum of Modern Art, New York/Scala, Florence. © The Easton Foundation/VAGA at ARS, NY and DACS, London 2022; 64 *Sulla fina anatomia degli organi centrali del sistema nervosa*, Camillo Golgi, 1885; 65 *Atlas d'embryologie*, Mathias Duval, 1889. Royal College of Physicians Edinburgh; 66 Courtesy Legado Cajal. Instituto Cajal (CSIC), Madrid; 67 The Museum of Modern Art, New York/Scala, Florence. © The Easton Foundation/VAGA at ARS, NY and DACS, London 2022; 68–71 Hamza Khan/Alamy Stock Photo; 72 Joost van den Bergh Ltd; 74 Courtesy Science History Institute, Philadelphia; 75 *Leviathan; or, The matter, forme, & power of a common-wealth, ecclesiasticall and civill*, Thomas Hobbes, 1651; 76 akg-images; 77 Line engraving by T. de Bry, 1617. Wellcome Collection, London; 78–79 Zentralbibliothek Zürich, Ms C 54 f28v, f29r, f41v, f42r; 80 *Theosophia Practica*, Johann Georg Gichtel,

1723. The Getty Research Institute, Los Angeles; 81 Joost van den Bergh Ltd; 82 Wellcome Collection, London; 83 Houghton Library. MS Typ 229. Grilandas inventum libri VI.; 84 British Library Board. All Rights Reserved/Bridgeman Images; 85 Artepics/Alamy Stock Photo; 86 Rubin Museum of Art, Gift of Shelley and Donald Rubin, C2006.66.509 (HAR 977); 87 Bhaktapur National Museum, Nepal; 88 *A Practical Treatise on Medical Diagnosis: For Students and Physicians*, John H. Musser, 1904; 89 *Psycho-Harmonial Philosophy*, Peter Pearson, 1910; 90 Karun Thakar Collection, London. Photo Desmond Brambley @desbrambley; 91 Los Angeles County Museum of Art. Purchased with funds provided by the Eli and Edythe Broad Foundation with additional funding by Jane and Terry Semel, the David Bohnett Foundation, Camilla Chandler Frost, Gayle and Edward P. Roski, and The Ahmanson Foundation; 92 *Inauguration of the Pleasure Dome*, Kenneth Anger, 1954; 93 Collection Musée National d'art Moderne, Centre Pompidou. Donation Bruno Decharme; 94 Yale Center for British Art, Paul Mellon Collection, New Haven, Connecticut, B1992.8.1(97); 95 The Picture Art Collection/Alamy Stock Photo; 96 Art Institute of Chicago, 1944.461; 97 Art Institute of Chicago, 1944.462; 98 *An Atlas of Anatomy*, Florence Fenwick Miller, London: Stanford, 1879; 99 *The Laws of Health*, Joseph C. Hutchison, 1884; 100 *A guide to operations on the brain*, Alec Fraser, New York, 1890; 101 Wellcome Collection, London; 102–103 Tibetan pattern book of proportions. Getty Research Institute, Los Angeles; 104–105 Los Angeles County Museum of Art. Purchased with funds provided by the Eli and Edythe Broad Foundation with additional funding by Jane and Terry Semel, the David Bohnett Foundation, Camilla Chandler Frost, Gayle and Edward P. Roski and The Ahmanson Foundation; 106 Smithsonian American Art Museum/Art Resource/Scala, Florence. © DACS 2022; 108 *Ioannis Keppleri Harmonices Mundi Libri V*, Johannes Kepler, 1619; 109 © F. L. C./ADAGP, Paris and DACS, London 2022; 110 *The mineral conchology of Great Britain*, James Sowerby, 1812; 111 Photo NYPL. © Vladimir Nabokov, used by permission of The Wylie Agency (UK) Limited; 112 Artist's © The Art Institute of Chicago. Chicago, IL. © 2022. The Art Institute

of Chicago/Art Resource, NY/Scala, Florence;
113 ullstein bild/Getty Images; 114 Historic
Illustrations/Alamy Stock Photo; 115
Minneapolis Institute of Art, The Walter
R. Bollinger Fund; 116 *British mineralogy,
or, Coloured figures intended to elucidate the
mineralogy of Great Britain*, James Sowerby,
1802; 117 Cinoby/Getty Images; 118 National
Gallery of Art, Washington, DC, Ailsa Mellon
Bruce Fund; 119 Photograph by Ingrid
Amslinger. Courtesy Hannsjörg Voth; 120
The Metropolitan Museum of Art, New York,
Mary Oenslager Fund, 2016; 121 Universitstats-
Bibliothek, Heidelberg, https://digi.ub.
uni-heidelberg.de/diglit/schoen1920;
122 David Rumsey Map Collection www.
davidrumsey.com ; 123, 124 Cornell University
Library; 125 PhotoStock-Israel/Alamy Stock
Photo; 126 Camille Delbos/Art In All of Us/
Corbis via Getty Images; 127 Herzog August
Bibliothek, Wolfenbüttel, 74–1–aug–2f;
128 The Metropolitan Museum of Art/Art
Resource/Scala, Florence; 129 *The Fourth
Dimension*, Charles Howard Hinton, London,
S. Sonnenschein & Co., 1906; 130 Universitäts-
bibliothek der LMU Munich, Cim. 103;
131 Laurent Millet, *Somnium* (Ref 5), 2015.
© Laurent Millet courtesy Catherine Edelman
Gallery, Chicago; 132 Veneranda Biblioteca
Ambrosiana/Mondadori Portfolio/Bridgeman
Images; 133 Heritage Image Partnership Ltd/
Alamy Stock Photo; 134 Herzog August
Bibliothek, Wolfenbüttel, 74–1–aug–2f;
135 *Vielecke und Vielflache: Theorie und
Geschichte*, Max Brückner, 1900; 136 M. C.
Escher, *Möbius Strip I*, 1961. © 2022 The
M. C. Escher Company-The Netherlands.
All rights reserved. www.mcescher.com; 137
The New York Public Library; 138 The Museum
of Modern Art, New York/Scala, Florence.
Courtesy The Estate of R. Buckminster Fuller;
139 *Chromatics, or An essay on the analogy and
harmony of colours*, George Field, 1817. Getty
Research Institute; 140 Raghvendra Sahai and
John Trauger (JPL), the WFPC2 science team,
and NASA; 141 © Emma Kunz Stiftung,
Würenlos; 142–143 Bibliothèque nationale de
France; 144 Courtesy of the George Eastman
Museum; 145 British Library Board. All Rights
Reserved/Bridgeman Images; 146 The National
Gallery of Denmark; 147 Library of Congress,
Washington, DC; 148 The Metropolitan
Museum of Art, New York, George Khuner
Collection, Bequest of Marianne Khuner,
1984; 149 John Mearman/Dreamstime.com;
150 Steve Alexander/Shutterstock; 151 Cooper
Hewitt, Smithsonian Design Museum,
Museum purchase through gift of various
donors and from Eleanor G. Hewitt Fund;
152 Science History Images/Alamy Stock
Photo; 153 Cooper Hewitt, Smithsonian Design
Museum, Gift of Gertrude W. Lewis; 154 The
Museum of Modern Art, New York/Scala,
Florence. © Man Ray 2015 Trust/DACS, London
2022; 155 © Gerhard Richter 2022 (0028);

156 Courtesy Wolfgang Beyer; 157 Courtesy
Ayreej Kanathil; 158 The Metropolitan Museum
of Art, New York. Gift of Mrs Russell Sage,
1910; 159 Albers Foundation/Art Resource,
NY. Photo Tim Nighswander. © The Josef and
Anni Albers Foundation/Artists Rights Society
(ARS), New York and DACS, London 2022;
160 Wellcome Collection, London; 161 Courtesy
Cavin-Morris Gallery. © Pauline Sunfly/
Copyright Agency. Licensed by DACS 2022;
162 Courtesy Jean-Pierre Dalbéra, on Flickr;
163 Art Institute of Chicago/akg-images;
164 The Metropolitan Museum of Art,
New York, Gift of Samuel P. Avery Jr, 1904;
166 The Cleveland Museum of Art, Gift of
Eugene and Joan Savitt in memory of Dr and
Mrs E. K. Zaworski, her grandparents 2006.203;
167 *Geheime Figuren der Rosenkreuzer*, Altona,
1785; 168 British Library Board. All Rights
Reserved/Bridgeman Images; 169 Rijksmuseum,
Amsterdam; 170 robertharding/Alamy Stock
Photo; 171 Bridgeman Images; 172 Mondadori
Portfolio/Electa/Sergio Anelli/Bridgeman
Images; 173a Quagga Media/Alamy Stock
Photo; 173b Courtesy Barry Lawrence
Ruderman Antique Maps Inc., raremaps.com;
174 Heritage Image Partnership Ltd/Alamy
Stock Photo; 175 Heritage Images/Getty
Images; 176–177 The Metropolitan Museum
of Art, New York. Harris Brisbane Dick
Fund, 1926; 178 Gilles Mermet/akg-images;
179 Herbert List/Magnum Photos; 180 Science
History Images/Alamy Stock Photo; 181,
182 Prahlad Bubbar, London; 183 Los Angeles
County Museum of Art. Purchased with
funds provided by Harry and Yvonne Lenart,
M.91.128.1; 184 Collection of Alexander Gorlizki;
185 *Biblia Pauperum*, Petrus I, Abbot of Metten,
Rabanus Maurus, Archbishop of Mainz,
1414 to 1415; 186 Joost van den Bergh Ltd;
187 Wellcome Collection, London; 188 The
Cleveland Museum of Art. Purchase and partial
gift from the Catherine and Ralph Benkaim
Collection; Severance and Greta Millikin
Purchase Fund 2018.201; 189 David Rumsey
Map Collection www.davidrumsey.com;
190 Biblioteca Civica Hortis, Trieste, Zoroaster
Clavis Artis, Ms–2–27, vol. 3, p. 116; 191 British
Library Board. All Rights Reserved/Bridgeman
Images; 192 Wellcome Collection, London;
193 The Metropolitan Museum of Art, New
York. Gift of John D. Rockefeller Jr, 1937;
194 Joost van den Bergh Ltd; 195 Wellcome
Collection, London; 196 Prahlad Bubbar,
London; 197 Yale University Library, New
Haven, Connecticut; 198 University of
Wisconsin, Madison. Libraries. Department
of Special Collections: Flat Shelving Duveen
D 897; 199 *A key to physic, and the occult sciences*,
Ebenezer Sibley, 1794. Leeds University
Archive; 200 Bibliothèque nationale de France;
201 National Gallery of Art, Washington, DC.
Samuel H. Kress Collection; 202 Courtesy
Vivienne Roberts; 203 Centre Pompidou,
MNAM-CCI, Dist. RMN-Grand Palais. Photo

Philippe Migeat. © ADAGP, Paris and DACS,
London 2022; 204–205 The J. Paul Getty
Museum, Los Angeles; 206 Rijksmuseum,
Amsterdam; 207 Library of Congress,
Washington, DC; 208 *Harmonia macrocosmica
sev atlas universalis et novus, totius universi
creati cosmographiam generalem, et novam
exhibens*, Andreas Cellarius, 1660; 210 *La
Cité de Diu* (Vol 1) by Augustine, translated
by Raoul de Presles, *c.* 1475; 211 David Rumsey
Map Collection www.davidrumsey.com;
212 *Harmonia macrocosmica sev atlas
universalis et novus, totius universi creati
cosmographiam generalem, et novam exhibens*,
Andreas Cellarius, 1660; 213 © The Royal
Society; 214 The Picture Art Collection/Alamy
Stock Photo; 215 Coloured engraving by J.
Chapman after V. Denon. Wellcome Collection,
London; 216–217 Bibliothèque nationale de
France; 218 Joost van den Bergh Ltd; 219
Courtesy of Karla Knight and Andrew Edlin
Gallery, NY; 220 Rubin Museum of Art,
C2009.9 (HAR 61200); 221 © 1930 Bruno
Munari. All rights reserved to Maurizio Corraini
s.r.l.; 222 Cheonsang Yeolcha Bunyajido, Seoul
Museum of History, Korea; 223 Courtesy Adler
Planetarium, Chicago, Illinois; 224 Augsburg
Book of Miracles, 1552; 225 Bayerische Staats-
bibliothek Munich, Cod.icon. 181, fol. 69r & 6r;
226 The J. Paul Getty Museum, Los Angeles,
Ms. Ludwig xv 4, fol. 148; 227 © Bodleian
Libraries, University of Oxford, MS. Douce 134,
fol. 49v; 228–229 BSB Shelfmark: Cod.icon.
340. Library of Congress, Washington, DC;
230–231 The Metropolitan Museum of Art,
New York, Gift of Herbert N. Straus, 1925;
232 *Astronomiæ instauratæ mechanica*, Tychonis
Brahe, 1598. The Royal Library, Copenhagen;
233 agefotostock/Alamy Stock Photo; 234
David Rumsey Map Collection www.david
rumsey.com; 235 *The story of the sun, moon,
and stars*, Agnes Giberne, 1898. Library of
Congress, Washington, DC; 236 *An original
theory or new hypothesis of the universe, founded
upon the laws of nature, and solving by
mathematical principles the general phænomena
of the visible creation; and particularly the via
lacteal*, Thomas Wright, 1750; 237 David
Rumsey Map Collection www.davidrumsey.
com; 238 Prisma Archivo/Alamy Stock Photo;
239 Augsburg Book of Miracles, 1552; 240
Roman Sigaev/Alamy Stock Photo; 241
Bibliothèque municipale de Bordeaux;
242 The Picture Art Collection/Alamy Stock
Photo; 243 The Metropolitan Museum of Art,
New York, The Elisha Whittelsey Collection,
The Elisha Whittelsey Fund, 1960; 244 Library
of Congress, Washington, DC; 245 *Milton's
Paradise Lost*, John Milton, Homer B. Sprague,
Boston, 1879; 246 David Rumsey Map
Collection www.davidrumsey.com; 247 *The
Beauty of the Heavens*, Charles F. Blunt, London,
1842; 248 Chicago and the Midwest (Newberry
Library). Rand McNally and Company records;
249 Field Museum Library/Getty Images.

Sources of Quotations

The Western Medical Tradition: 800 BC to AD 1800 (Cambridge: Cambridge University Press, 1995), p. 337

102 Cited in Alma E. Cavazos-Gaither and Carl C. Gaither (eds), *Gaither's Dictionary of Scientific Quotations* (New York: Springer, 2012), p. 104

104 Kumalau Tawali, 'The Old Woman's Message', *Signs in the Sky* (Port Moresby: Papua Pocket Poets, 1970)

CHAPTER 3

107 Cited in Christopher B. Kaiser, *Creational Theology and the History of Physical Science* (Leiden: Brill, 1997), p. 168

110 Vladimir Nabokov, 'Butterflies: On Life as a Lepidopterist', *The New Yorker* (12 June 1948); www.newyorker.com

112 Cited in Britta Benke, *Georgia O'Keefe 1887–1986: Flowers in the Desert* (Cologne: Taschen, 2003), p. 57

115 Chippendale armorial bookplate for Erasmus Darwin (1771), British Museum, London

116 George Cuvier, *Georges Cuvier, Fossil Bones, and Geological Catastrophes: New Translations and Interpretations of the Primary Texts*, trans. Martin J. S. Rudwick (Chicago: University of Chicago Press, 2008), p. 205

121 Nikola Tesla, 'The Problem of Increasing Human Energy', *The Century Magazine* (June 1900), pp. 175–211

125 Jorge Luis Borges, 'The Garden of the Forking Paths', *Labyrinths: Selected Stories and Other Writings* (New York: New Directions, 1964)

128 Cited in George Webster, 'The little cube that changed the world', *CNN* (11 Oct. 2012), www.edition.cnn.com

130 Cited in Stephanie Frank Singer, *Symmetry in Mechanics: A Gentle, Modern Introduction* (Boston: Birkhäuser, 2004), p. 6

133 Wilson O. Clough, 'Poetry and Painting: A Study of Parallels between the Two Arts', *College Art Journal*, vol. 18, no. 2 (Winter, 1959), pp. 117–29

134 Ralph Waldo Emerson, *The Poems of Ralph Waldo Emerson*, vol. 9 (Boston; New York: Houghton, Mifflin and Company, 1904); Bartleby, www.bartleby.com

138 Buckminster Fuller, Jerome Agel and Quentin Fiore, *I Seem to Be a Verb* (Berkeley: Gingko Press Inc., 2015)

140 Cited in Ivy Bedworth, *Rationalising the Bible*, vol. 1 (Howick, SA: Bedworth, 2016), p. 55

144 Zach Mortice, 'Sun, Soil, Spirit: The Architecture of Mario Botta', *American Institute of Architects* (2008), https://info.aia.org

146 Robert Frost; The Poetry Foundation, www.poetryfoundation.org

149 John Milton, 'At a Vacation Exercise in the College', *The Complete Poems*, vol. 4, ed. Charles W. Eliot (New York: P. F. Collier & Son, 1909–14); Bartleby, www.bartleby.com

152 Katherine Mansfield, letter to Dorothy Brett, July 1921, *Katherine Mansfield Letters and Journals: A Selection*, ed. C. K. Stead (New Zealand: Penguin, 1977)

154 Guy Murchie, *The Seven Mysteries of Life: An Exploration in Science & Philosophy* (New York: Houghton Mifflin Harcourt, 1999), p. 58

158 Cited in Barbara Teller Ornelas and Lynda Teller Pete, 'Spider Woman's Children: The next generation of Navajo weavers', *Garland Magazine* (5 Dec. 2019), www.garlandmag.com

161 Cited in Diana James 'Tjukurpa' Time' (2005), *Long History, Deep Time: Deepening Histories of Place*, eds Ann McGrath and Mary Anne Jebb (Canberra: Anu Press, 2015), p. 33

INTRODUCTION

9 Cited in Derek and Julia Parker, *Parkers' Encyclopedia of Astrology* (London: Watkins Publishing, 2012)

13 Hildegard von Bingen, *Meditations with Hildegard of Bingen*, ed. Gabriele Uhlien (Rochester, VT: Bear & Company, 1983), p. 41

15 Marcus Aurelius, *The Meditations*, trans. George Long, book 4; The Internet Classics Archive, http://classics.mit.edu

27 John Milton, *Paradise Lost*, 2nd edn, ed. Scott Elledge (New York: W. W. Norton & Company, 1993), book IX

31 Thomas Taherne, *Centuries of Meditations*, ed. Bertram Dobell (London: Dobell, 1908)

33 Yamaguchi Sodo, *Haiku*, vol. 2, trans. R. H. Blyth (Tokyo: Hokuseiko, 1950), p. 34; The Haiku Foundation, www.thehaikufoundation.org

CHAPTER 1

35 William Blake; The Poetry Foundation, www.poetryfoundation.org

40 Nathaniel Hawthorn, *The House of Seven Gables* (Cambridge, MA: The Riverside Press, 1913), p. 34

45 William Heyen, *The Swastika Poems* (New York: Vanguard Press, 1977)

47 Annie Dillard, *An American Childhood* (Edinburgh: Canongate, 2016)

50 Percy Bysshe Shelley; The Poetry Foundation, www.poetryfoundation.org

55 Charles Darwin, *The Variation of Animals and Plants Under Domestication*, vol. 2 (New York: Organe Judd, 1868), p. 204

59 Victor Hugo, *Les Misérables*, vol. 3, trans. Charles E. Wilbour (New York: Carleton, 1862), book 3, ch. 3, p. 41; HathiTrust Digital Library, https://babel.hathitrust.org

61 Matsuo Bashō, *Haiku*, vol. 1, p. 267

65 Hugo, *Les Misérables*, vol. 3, book 3, ch. 3, p. 41

68 Leonardo da Vinci, *The Notebooks of Leonardo da Vinci*, vol. 2 (New York: Dover Publications Inc., 1970), p. 220

71 Rudolf Arnheim, *Parables of Sun Light*, (Berkeley: University of California Press, 1989), p. 160

CHAPTER 2

73 Cited in R. C. Zaehner, *Zurvan: A Zoroastrian Dilemma* (New York: Biblio & Tannen, 1972), p. 145

82 da Vinci, *The Notebooks*, p. 221

91 Fritjof Capra, *The Tao of Physics: An Exploration of the Parallels Between Modern Physics and Eastern Mysticism* (Boston: Shambhala, 2010)

93 Cited in Maturin Murray Ballou, *Treasury of Thought: Forming an Encyclopædia of Quotations from Ancient and Modern Authors* (Cambridge, MA: The Riverside Press, 1894), p. 5

94 William Blake, *Jerusalem*, plate 77, 'To The Christians…' (1804–20), Yale Centre for British Art, Paul Mellon Collection

96 Cited in Lawrence I. Conrad et al.,

CHAPTER 4

165 Zain Hashmi, *A Blessed Olive Tree: A Spiritual Journey in Twenty Short Stories* (Create Space, 2017)

168 Milton, *Paradise Lost*, book IV

173 Isaac Watts, Psalm 68, pt 2, www.hymnary.org

175 The Bible, Matthew 25:41, the Bible, New International Version, www.biblehub.com

176 Milton, *Paradise Lost*, book I

179 Homer, *The Iliad*, trans. Martin Hammond (London: Penguin, 1987), book 11, l. 36

185 Kalidasa, *Translations of Shakuntala, and Other Works*, trans. Arthur W. Ryder (New Delhi: Prabhat Prakashan, 1914)

186 Friedrich Nietzsche, *Thus Spoke Zarathustra*, ed. and trans. Adrian Del Caro, ed. Robert Pippin (Cambridge: Cambridge University Press, 2006), p. 175

188 'Divisions of Naraka', *The Vishnu Purana*, trans. H. H. Wilson (1840)

192 Cited in Odell Shepard, *The Lore of the Unicorn* (London: George Allen & Unwin, 1930)

195 Emerson, *The Poems of Ralph Waldo Emerson*

196 Philippe de Thaon, *The Bestiary of Philippe de Thaon*, ed. Thomas Wright (London: The Historical Society, 1841); The Medieval Bestiary, www.bestiary.ca

203 Hildegard von Bingen, *Selected Writings*, trans. Mark Atherton (London: Penguin, 2005)

205 Cited in Randall Lesaffer, *European Legal History: A Cultural and Political Perspective* (Cambridge: Cambridge University Press, 2009), p. 95

CHAPTER 5

209 Walt Whitman, *Leaves of Grass* (Philadelphia: David McKay, 1891–92)

212 Hugo, *Les Misérables*, vol. 3, book 3, ch. 3, p. 41

216 Cited in Jean-Pierre Lasota (ed.), *Astronomy at the Frontiers of Science* (Netherlands: Springer, 2011), p. 291

218 Ralph Waldo Emerson, *Ralph Waldo Emerson: The Major Poetry*, ed. Albert J. von Frank (Cambridge, MA: The Belknap Press, 2015), p. 188

223 Cited in Richard Tarnas, *Cosmos and Psyche: Intimations of a New World View* (New York: Penguin, 2006)

224 Nietzsche, *Thus Spoke Zarathustra*, p. 175

227 Cited in Marco Piccolino and Nicholas J. Wade, *Galileo's Visions: Piercing the Spheres of the Heavens by Eye and Mind* (Oxford: Oxford University Press, 2014), p. 52

228 Milton, *Paradise Lost*, book VII

233 Cited in Nancy Atkinson, 'Rosetta Meets Astroid Lutetia', *Universe Today* (12 July 2010), www.universetoday.com

235 John Keats; The Poetry Foundation, www.poetryfoundation.org

237 Cited in Cavazos-Gaither, *Gaither's Dictionary of Scientific Quotations*, p. 1478

238 Philippe Jaccottet, *Words in the Air*, trans. Derek Mahon (Loughcrew, IE: Gallery Books, 1998)

240 Omar Khayyam, *Rubaiyat of Omar Khayyam*, trans. Edward Fitzgerald (Boston: Branden Publishing Co., 1989)

242 *Völuspá*, trans. Henry Adam Bellows (1936), verse 5; www.voluspa.org

247 Cited in Douglas Botting, *Gerald Durrell: An Authorized Biography* (London: HarperCollins, 2000), p. xvii

248 Tesla, 'The Problem of Increasing Human Energy'

ACKNOWLEDGMENTS

256 Emily Dickinson, *The Complete Poems of Emily Dickinson*, ed. Thomas H. Johnson (Boston: Little, Brown & Company, 1960)

Index

Acknowledgments

'A Vastness, as a Neighbor, came,
A Wisdom, without Face, or Name,
A Peace, as Hemispheres at Home
And so the Night became.'

Emily Dickinson, 'The Crickets sang' (1104), *c.* 1866

This book is dedicated to Jackie, a constant star
in a time of chaos, darkness and mischief. x

I would like to thank Jane Laing, Phoebe Lindsley,
Florence Allard, Tristan de Lancey, Sadie Butler and
everyone at Thames & Hudson involved in the realization
of this long-cherished project. I am incredibly grateful
to all of you for your invaluable contributions, insights
and encouragement, and for your patience and support
during turbulent times.

I would also like to express my deep gratitude to all
the artists, galleries, museums, institutions and estates
who have so generously granted us permission to feature
their work – the book would not exist without them.

ABOUT THE AUTHOR

Renowned image alchemist Stephen Ellcock is a
London-based curator, writer, researcher and online
collector of images who has spent the last decade creating
an ever-expanding virtual museum of art that is open
to all via social media. His ongoing attempt at creating
the ultimate social media 'Cabinet of Curiosities' has
so far attracted more than 600,000 followers worldwide.

He is also the author of *All Good Things*, *The Book
of Change*, *England On Fire*, with text by Mat Osman,
and *Jeux de Mains*, a collaboration with Cécile
Poimboeuf-Koizumi.

307 illustrations

FRONT COVER *Lichtenberg Figures: A. R. von Hippel*,
György Kepes, 1951. Courtesy of the Department
of Special Collections, Stanford University Libraries
and the estate of György Kepes.

BACK COVER & PAGE 2 Illustrations from *Eclipses
luminarium*, Cyprian Leowitz, 1555. Bayerische
Staatsbibliothek Munich, Cod.icon. 181, fol.69r & 6r.

SPINE & ENDPAPERS Marbled paper
from the collection of Richard Sheaff.

PAGE 1 *Saturn Return*, Pola Von Grüt, 2019.

First published in the United Kingdom in 2022
by Thames & Hudson Ltd, 181A High Holborn,
London WC1V 7QX

First published in the United States of America in 2022
by Thames & Hudson Inc., 500 Fifth Avenue,
New York, New York 10110

Reprinted 2024

The Cosmic Dance © 2022 Thames & Hudson Ltd,
London

Text © 2022 Stephen Ellcock

For image copyright information see pages 252–253

Designed by Daniel Streat, Visual Fields

British Library Cataloguing-in-Publication Data
A catalogue record for this book is available from
the British Library

Library of Congress Control Number 2022932115

ISBN 978-0-500-25253-6

Printed and bound in China by
C&C Offset Printing Co. Ltd

Be the first to know about our new releases,
exclusive content and author events by visiting
thamesandhudson.com
thamesandhudsonusa.com
thamesandhudson.com.au

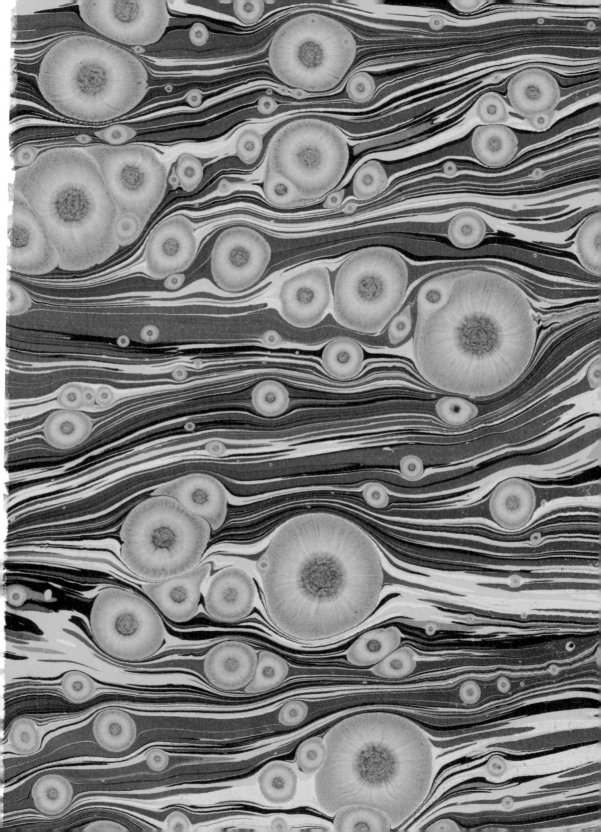

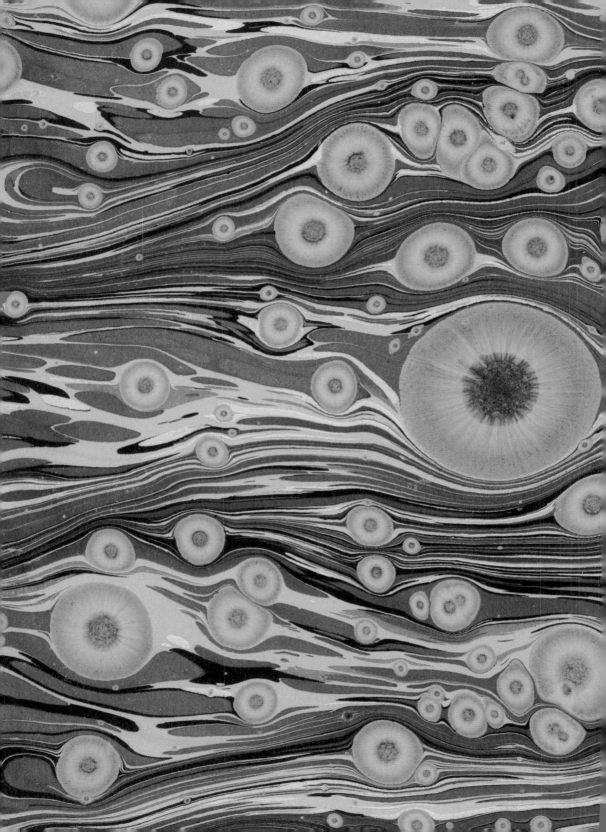